It Sort of Clicks

IAN BOTHAM
PETER ROEBUCK

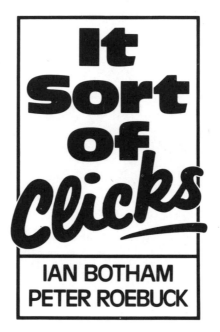

It Sort of Clicks

IAN BOTHAM
PETER ROEBUCK

WILLOW BOOKS
Collins
8 Grafton Street, London W1
1987

Willow Books
William Collins Sons & Co. Ltd
London · Glasgow · Sydney · Auckland
Toronto · Johannesburg

First published in hardback 1986
Reprinted 1986
First published in paperback 1987
© Newschoice Ltd/Peter Roebuck 1986, 1987

BRITISH LIBRARY CATALOGUING IN PUBLICATION DATA
Botham, Ian
It sort of clicks: Ian Botham talking to
Peter Roebuck. – 2nd rev. ed.
1. Botham, Ian   2. Cricket players –
England – Biography
I. Title   II. Roebuck, Peter, 1956–
796.35′8′0924   GV915.B58

ISBN 0 00 218292 0

Photoset in Century Schoolbook by
Rowland Phototypesetting Ltd
Bury St Edmunds, Suffolk
Made and printed in Great Britain by
Robert Hartnoll (1985) Ltd, Bodmin

Contents

Warm-Up

Biography, according to Michael Holroyd, began as a form of praise. In cricket, an illusion was created of a noble game played by upstanding men, an illusion founded upon sympathetic character studies.

In the last few years our cricketing heroes have been examined with greater sincerity. At last we need not accept that our game was always conducted on a higher plane than the rest of existence. At last we can judge the present in the light of a history which contains both good and bad, rather than as a story of alarming decency flawed by one deplorable episode (Larwood trying to bang a few Australian heads). Bodyline has been portrayed as a solitary fall from grace – as if Mary Poppins had gone out boozing with Marlene Dietrich for the night. Instead, with the advent of modern, realistic studies, cricket is presented as a game played, even then, by ordinary men.

Since David Foot's biography of the 'tortured genius' of Somerset, Gimblett, a stream of books has been written about prickly characters. C. B. Fry, whose own autobiography was entitled *A Life Worth Living*, has been presented as a man whose life after cricket was curiously dispiriting. Percy Chapman, the smiling emperor, died a drunken embarrassment to his friends. Harold Gimblett, champion of the west, was an awkward, depressed man who took his own life. Jardine, less disturbingly, felt that he had been betrayed by authority.

Hammond's haughty coldness has been exposed. Parker, Parkin and MacBryan have been portrayed as cussed men poorly treated by their establishments. These revelations provide a refreshing insight into cricket's past.

Of course the very reason for writing about some of these men was that they were vain or arrogant or truculent, and as such were not typical. Nevertheless, the portraits of Fry, Chapman and Gimblett in particular shed light upon a history we had been encouraged to regard as inspirational.

Whether or not the 'villain' of our age, Ian Botham, is so realistically portrayed is a matter of opinion. Certainly his weaknesses are open to public scrutiny and his triumphs well documented, but this does not necessarily help to broaden our understanding of his character.

Thirty years ago, Botham's private life would not have been so lasciviously scoured. Scandals were scarcely mentioned. In *Unholy Trinity* (profiles of Charlie Parker, Cecil Parkin and Jack MacBryan), David Foot reports that everyone chuckled when a batsman, already bowled, knocked down his remaining stumps. In *46 Not Out* Robertson-Glasgow describes a fast bowler who deliberately ran into the umpire – he apparently 'replaced his teeth' and the game continued. Such matters were included as amusing asides, as the sort of thing that happened in the heat of the moment and was best forgotten. In 1986, journalists write sermons about far less.

It is no longer universally supposed that cricket represents all the requisite manly virtues; cricketers, it is realized, are as rum a set of beggars as any other. What is more, cricketers from the golden age – which appears to stretch from Bob Barber to Arthur Shrewsbury – weren't that different either. Botham may not be such a contrast to Miller or Armstrong after all.

If the players are much the same, the game itself has changed. Bouncers are bowled to tailenders and people don't walk as often – but the Australians, realizing the hypocrisy of spasmodic 'walking', never did much anyway. There are more fast bowlers, and more short deliveries; the game is more ruthless. Still, the greengrocer on the corner has gone, and so has the Sunday postal service and *Dixon of Dock Green* too. At least now one can compare realities, rather than a grim present with a grand past.

CHAPTER ONE

The Great
White Hope

He walked from John o' Groats to Land's End, and thumped a policeman when he got there. He popped off to Hollywood, where he was out for a duck, ignored by the movie moguls. He has appeared in court several times and been involved in a libel case. He has a wife, three children, a few racehorses and two enormous dogs. He wants to fly round the world but can't because he is colour-blind. He has played football for Scunthorpe and snooker for his pub team. He has been England's hero on the cricket field times without number. Ian Botham is an unusual man.

Writing about Botham is not easy. It is hard to add muscle and sinew to his image as a comic-strip hero. His life, at least as defined in the newspapers, swings from devilry to sainthood. He hardly ever appears as a mortal. Moreover, any book about Ian is bound to be out of date, at least in terms of his deeds. In the months between the ink drying and the book appearing he might have gone to prison, climbed Everest or ridden in the Grand National (on a particularly strong horse).

Ian's walk, on which he raised £710,000 for leukaemia research, was an incredible idea, magnificently executed. Cynics regarded it as a public relations exercise but it was nothing of the sort. Botham was mesmerized by the notion of striding from Scotland to Land's End. It was a romantic idea, an indulgence even, a sacrifice only in part.

Ian wants to be a hero to the young and he loves the way

kids emulate his bravado. He wants children to admire him and to be inspired by him. He is determined to stay youthful, to enjoy himself. He yearns for the freedom to drop everything to go on a walk, even to cross the Himalayas on an elephant. Who would ever have thought of that? What a lark! The fuddy-duddies will shake their heads, but then they always do. Isn't that half the fun?

Really Ian is a character from Smollett or Fielding. He doesn't give a damn: he wants to ride a horse, down a pint, roar around the land waking up the sleepers, show them things can be done. As it is, he has to play cricket all the time and worry about newspapermen, a Gulliver tied down to the little people.

In the West Indies in 1985–86 he was once again in the news. He bowled poorly and failed to reach 50. He gambled, relied upon flair, inspiration and luck, and did not improve on his rather mediocre record against the West Indies. He is sensitive to this weakness, for it alone allows those who decry his stature to persevere in their argument. If only he could score that elusive hundred . . . So often Ian's friends find themselves saying 'If only the damned fellow would . . .' His poor form added to the pressures upon him, and he was scarcely out of the headlines. If it wasn't drugs, it was reckless batting. Stories about Botham sell newspapers; with his fine want of discretion he promises stories. It is as simple as that.

It is a shame that instead of enjoying Botham's gifts of life and laughter, we write about his mistakes. Arriving exhausted in Cornwall, Ian apparently thumped a policeman. Let it pass. He was accused of meddling with drugs. Let it pass. Harm is done not by the deed but by its unkind exposure. Let the stone throwers raise £710,000, let them bring the joy which Botham brought in 1981. They are a miserable lot.

In October 1985 Botham resigned as Somerset's captain. He had been away too much, throughout the winter, often in the summer too. His team had lost several of its best players and the youngsters were just beginning their careers. Ian had taken only 11 championship wickets in 1985 and had appeared frustrated by injuries and defeats. Only at the crease, smashing sixes in the river, was he his old self. At times he finds county cricket a chore, returning from a tour or a Test exhausted only to realize that everyone expects him to bowl brilliantly and bat magnificently. Supervising a group of twenty professional cricketers as well was too much.

Ian was sorry to lose his position, particularly as it appeared that some of his friends in his home club were turning on him. It was not so, of course, yet it was impossible to prevent his resignation being presented in this light. Temporarily he must have felt like an outcast from his own family. But my appointment as his successor did not alter his attitude to me, and we quickly resumed our consideration of the mysteries of his career.

How had this larrikin from Yeovil turned into such an awesome cricketer? That was the puzzle. No one had picked him at seventeen, yet two years later he was with the greats. This theme flowed through our conversations. How had this fame affected him? Was he bored? What about these cavalier clothes, and these films? Asked if he would rather appear in a movie or hit sixes against the Australians, Ian replied that he had already cracked lots of sixes and fancied a change. Such an attitude horrifies cricket followers. Ian is a man who is forever seeking fresh sensations. He has played cricket for twelve years yet he has also played soccer, flown with the Red Arrows, driven fast cars, gone fishing. He wanted to try parachuting but they wouldn't let him. If ever he becomes a movie star, well, that will convince people he is not some yobbo from Yeovil.

Botham does not belong to cricket. He is a man with a life to lead, believing that it is better to burn out than to fade away. Nothing would be more horrible to him than playing as a grumpy old professional of thirty-eight. Let his star flash across our horizon, let it illuminate our skies, and then let it disappear.

Ian's career appears to be on the wane in any case, those mercurial sixes notwithstanding. He is still a magnificent cricketer, still a player of bravado, but those sixes were an echo of an image. At his best, he would have grabbed the ball and demolished the opposition, or at least he would have had a go. In 1985 he was tired, he found it all too much bloody effort. He seemed to have had enough. Now he speaks of retiring from Test cricket. He condemns the invasions of his privacy which prevent him from living freely.

At thirty, Ian has passed beyond his dreams (and he is an imaginative fellow). It irritates him that, despite his incredible career, he is still often regarded as a muddied oaf. Perhaps that is why he wanted to do this book, with someone who has known him from those innocent early days. He didn't want to be regarded always as a villain, he wanted to explain himself to those with sympathetic ears. Few sportsmen want to end their days in the chamber of horrors. Only Boycott seems utterly unconcerned about his image and, of course, he is a hero in parts of Yorkshire and everyone else is prejudiced and does not understand. People like Connors, Close, Trueman, Muhammad Ali, Billie Jean King and, I'll wager, McEnroe and Navratilova, begin as sharks and end as dolphins. They want to be recognized as great players, that is the drive which lifts them to the top – they want to be the best. After a few years at their peak they feel their powers fading, or they are bored, and they begin to yearn for sympathy. They want to be admired at first but in the end they want to be loved. This book is a part of Ian's campaign to rebuild his reputation.

In our conversations, Ian did not want to recollect but to explain. This was convenient, because what is most interesting about him is how this apparently ordinary lad has developed into an all-rounder of such prodigious power and, more particularly, how he has survived the outrageous expectations we

8

have of him. The truth, of course, is that Botham is not an ordinary fellow. It is beyond the capacity and the imagination of ordinary fellows to stretch as far as Botham has stretched.

What emerged from our conversations? That Botham's foremost quality is his courage. That his fame has inhibited him. One of Botham's friends is George Best, a soccer player of genius who, like Botham, has a self-destructive streak in him, an inability to calculate his moves within his own interests. Ian lacks Best's smiling charm, but he, too, lives a frantic, unbalanced, unplanned life. He, too, is a gambler who will be cherished while his luck holds. Botham's life is wildly exciting. He cannot endure days without sparkle, and if he is bored with his cricket he will search elsewhere for inspiration.

Not all top sportsmen live like Caligula but it is quite possible to do so. Countless rock stars have destroyed themselves with drugs, lots of gifted games players have fallen by the way in a cloud of alcohol. It is hardly surprising. They enter a world full of excitement, their egos are boosted, they want to lay on a bit of the flash. Maybe, too, they stop believing so much in what they do for a living, maybe the satisfaction fades as the years go by, maybe the rewards pale by comparison with the easy highs available to the successful. Few have the discipline or maturity or simple plain dullness to ignore the trappings of superstardom.

Ian *is* a great star, one of the most famous people in England. This elevation has had an effect on his character. He is an unusually lonely man. He would never admit it for he refuses to tolerate anything negative, but he surrounds himself with loyal friends and will not go anywhere without them. Somewhere inside he is unsure, threatened by the world. He is street-wise rather than highly intelligent, tactically sound rather than a judge of character and sometimes he feels a little out of his depth. He enjoys the vast notoriety which surrounds him, a mixture of Churchill and Ned Kelly, but he is vulnerable too and likes to escape to remote Scottish rivers to fish.

His real home is with his friends, almost exclusively male, who form a web around him. Ian employs one friend, Andy Withers, as his helper; really, though, his duties are many. He is a guarantee that a male will always be on hand. Another good friend, John Border, Allan's brother, accompanied Ian on his epic walk. He, too, is a sturdy character who will not sit around moaning about Ian's faults or lecture him on self-improvement. He can play golf, drink, shoot or whatever with his mate. There are a few others – friends from football, friends from early days in Yeovil. Fame has driven Ian towards these close friends. Viv Richards is another. At Somerset he has a couple of colleagues who are dear to his heart and towards them he is utterly loyal, to the point of unfairness towards others.

In New Zealand in 1984 he spent most of his time with Elton John. Some years earlier, on his first tour in 1978, he had passed many nights in the company of Lever and Willis, drinking pints and admiring the young ladies as they wandered by. The contrast is a vital one. In 1984 Botham attached himself to Elton's group and shared their evenings, their very different experiences. In some respects Ian and Elton have much in common. Both have been forced into false, self-absorbed worlds by their success. Botham's room in Epworth is lined with photographs, autograph sheets, balls and bats – reminders of his triumphs. It is *his* room, a tribute to himself. At his parties, Elton John entertains his guests by playing his own songs. Each man celebrates his own achievements, as if to bolster up his vanity, as if they might disappear if they are ignored.

Botham and Elton have one other thing in common, possibly the most dangerous thing of all: they have both made it. What in Ian's life can ever match the triumphs of 1981? Does such excitement lead a man to want more of the same, so that he becomes addicted to the highs? Botham's life has been extraordinarily packed with dramas, but he must know that

1981 was his peak. No wonder he surrounds himself with mementoes of those glories. As soldiers returning from war feel listless, without the charge of danger, so too do some Welsh rugby players, who have known the choirs of Cardiff Arms Park; they find it difficult to adjust to a quieter life. It is not surprising that the beefy lad from Yeovil finds friendship with Elton John. They have fears in common.

Ian has not lost his enjoyment of simple things and at times he yearns to return to those reckless teenage days when no one gave a damn what he did. He is deeply grateful to any colleague who invites him out to the pub for a drink, to anyone who accompanies him on a night out somewhere. He loves to play soccer, darts, snooker with the boys. Sometimes this gratitude is almost embarrassing – certainly you realize that Ian's great notoriety, his *Boy's Own* heroism, has made him lonely.

Botham is neither a warm, cuddly bear (as is sometimes imagined) nor a nasty, violent man. He is an unusual man of immensely powerful character, a man full of life who has become slightly remote and introverted, but also ruthless, as a result of his career. He is a generous man too, with an abiding loyalty to those who have stuck with him. Only a part of what drives him is revealed here, though perhaps a greater part than most top sportsmen are willing to reveal.

We had intended to present this book as a series of conversations between us, but we found this style to be too cumbersome. Accordingly, most of my opinions are reserved for the introductions which begin each chapter, while Ian's words appear almost as he spoke them. He did not need to be goaded. This was a book he wanted to do and this was the way he wanted to do it.

One more thing must be said. In this book Ian explains how much he enjoys living in Epworth. This was not a public relations exercise – he meant every word. A few months later the police raided his house in Epworth and charged him with possessing cannabis resin. He pleaded guilty and accepted his punishment, expressing regret that he had damaged himself in the eyes of youngsters. Friends told him that he had been betrayed by someone in the village, the village where he believed he was understood. He concluded that he could not stay in Epworth, though the vast majority of people there were still his friends. He decided to sell his house and to move to some more remote part of Yorkshire.

Ian's Story

I've toured New Zealand and Pakistan twice, seven years apart. My experiences on these two tours were totally different. I don't suppose either country had changed much, the changes were in me. Some of them were forced by my position and by my reputation, others by my preference.

On my first tour I roomed with J. K. Lever. He was an experienced player and could show the new fellow the ropes. We were good mates because J. K. has a sense of fun and enjoys a beer as much as I do. He thought I was going to be a nuisance, shouting my mouth off, living like a maniac, but in the end he said I'd learned a lot and we've been close friends ever since. On these international tours you either learn quickly or hate every moment. Some people don't like it – Mike Gatting is an example – because suddenly you're a junior player. At your county you are senior, you bowl down the wind, field where you choose and have lots of younger lads under you. Suddenly someone else is telling you what to do, sending you on errands and dropping you.

At Somerset I was the main bowler – we hardly had anyone else – and under Brearley in Pakistan I was a novice. I was supposed to hold my tongue and to respect my elders and betters so that I could learn from them. I wasn't much good at that. I wanted to mix with the senior players. Instead of earning their friendship I took it for granted. They thought I was a big-headed little sod, a bit like Brian Close on his first tour to Australia. I was brash, I didn't pretend to be humble, I didn't sit at the feet of the great men asking them how they bent their left knees so nicely. I didn't fit in, I wasn't really an England player in terms of conduct or concentration. The others thought I fooled around. People in Somerset knew I could be an idiot but they knew I was a hell of a competitor too. In that first month in Pakistan Brearley could see only this crazy lad who said he could do this or that or the other and who showed no great respect for the senior players. I didn't even take Boycott seriously, and he was a god, apparently. You weren't supposed to tease Geoffrey. It wasn't my cup of tea at all. Too much of a hierarchy. In cricket you're on the field together and everyone's equal.

For a month I was pretty well ignored, and felt left out. I suppose it is usually so with youngsters, especially those who are regarded as a threat. I'm the same now – some lad comes in for his first match and prances around like he's got a sticky bun up his backside and I want to knock his head off. Probably I'd have treated myself badly too. Young players are supposed to be seen and not heard.

Brearley thought I was an oaf for a long time. I don't think he was prepared for a hulking lad from Yeovil who wanted to conquer the world. He is a fellow for symphonies, for slow and thoughtful music. He likes meditating and working people out. In me he saw only a wild youth who wouldn't do as he was told. He thought I was undisciplined, vulgar and crude. For several months he treated me with something approaching contempt. He wasn't alone; a lot of people were wary of me. I was friends with Willis, Hendrick and Lever, and they are still my friends.

Neither Hendrick nor I played in the later Test matches because we were ill. We tried to pretend we were fit for one, so Brearley said 'Run round the ground'. Hendrick took two paces and collapsed. I ran halfway round this massive stadium in Lahore and then the world went weird. I didn't play for eight weeks. I haven't been sick or injured since.

Really I feel I should have played early in the tour, but I hardly played at all. It was very frustrating. They kept picking fast bowlers who were wasting their time on those featherbed pitches. In Pakistan the wickets are just rolled mud: no grass at all, just shining mud. Neither Pakistan nor India had any fast bowlers for this reason yet Brearley kept choosing two for every game!

It is odd that these nations have so few fast bowlers. It isn't a matter of physique or of courage – the Indians and Pakistanis are some of the bravest, toughest warriors in the world. You can't tell me these people cannot bowl fast. They can't see the sense in it, that's the point. Yet Brearley kept leaving out his all-rounders and choosing men to rush in and bang the ball down. Mad dogs, Englishmen and Cambridge philosophers, that's what I thought.

I'm convinced Brearley stopped me playing in Pakistan. He wanted to dominate everything and he was disturbed that this loudmouth from Somerset didn't gaze at him as if he was Moses. We had a row during a one-day international. I was just recovering from the dysentery that Mike Hendrick and I had suffered from. I was at mid-wicket and the ball went to deep cover. I didn't know which end to back up. I chose one and the throw came in. I found Brearley standing behind me. He wanted to know why the hell I wasn't at the other end. I told him that I didn't have eyes in the back of my head. He said that I always had an answer. And I said: 'Well, perhaps I was bloody well right for once.' That was the end of it, and the game carried on. I wasn't upset because it was all in the heat of the moment but Brearley was. A few weeks later I realized I wasn't getting a fair go. So I went to Brearley and said so. He said that Chris Old was a better all-rounder. I told him I'd prove him wrong.

It was only when Brearley's arm was broken and he arrived

in New Zealand as a journalist that he bothered with me at all. Boycott was in charge and suddenly Brearley could see me in a different way, not as a truculent youth but as a spirited cricketer. We spent some evenings together, drinking wine and chatting. After I'd scored 150 and taken 8 wickets in a Test he said, 'Well maybe you have got Chris Old covered.' We laughed about it and had a few dinners together. People misunderstood our relationship. They regarded him as an uncle taking care of a wild youth. We were much more equal than that, right from the start. I'm not a fellow who listens to many people or who needs guidance. I have immense confidence. Brearley and I were friends. We liked each other, it was as simple as that.

Pakistan wasn't really the place for me in 1977 – it has never brought me much luck. (Don't worry, I won't mention my mother-in-law – who is, by the way, delightful!) New Zealand was much better. I was nearly a stone lighter when we left Lahore. As our plane took off there was a spontaneous cheer from everyone, players and management alike. It was astounding. Probably it was the thought of fresh steaks and cold beer which raised our spirits. Tours to Moslem countries are rarely much fun for an Englishman! Not that all Pakistanis are bad. Abdul Qadir is an interesting bloke; he takes his prayer mat with him wherever he goes. He's from an ordinary background whereas most of his colleagues are rich – except Javed, who comes from humble origins, which is one reason some of his colleagues are reluctant to accept his authority. You can't understand a word Abdul says, and he dresses scruffily. They wouldn't let him into the ground on his Test debut because he was wearing sandshoes and jeans. Most of the others wear silk.

Majid is a Moslem too, a man with a deep voice, much more religious than the Indians who include all sorts of faiths (Hindu, Christian, Moslem and, I dare say, the odd non-believer). When Pakistan resumed Test cricket against India, Majid treated it as a religious war. It wasn't India versus Pakistan, it was Hindu versus Moslem: Northern Ireland all over again. Maybe we should stop national cricket and start playing religious cricket. There would be a hell of a lot more bumpers bowled, and you wouldn't be able to trust the umpires but it would be interesting! All the West Indians are religious – many of them say prayers when they go to bed. Richards and Haynes both cross themselves when they score a century, thanking God for his help. Wessels does the same, though I'm not convinced his God looks much like Viv Richards's!

New Zealand suited me well. I made my name there. I forced my way into the Test team in Canterbury. Either Gatting or myself was to be chosen. He is not a good player of spin, or he wasn't then anyway, though he did manage to hit Somerset for 258 at Bath in 1984! He was stumped early on so I went in. I had a bit of luck, I played forward and the ball rolled back and missed my off-stump by a whisker. Sometimes there isn't much between triumph and disaster. I ended up with 126 not out and played in the Tests. We lost the first, won the second and the third was a tame draw. I don't think it made any difference that Brearley wasn't captain. I'd still have had my chance. Mind you, I always thought that Brearley tended to favour his Middlesex colleagues. I suppose that's understandable really, because you see more of them, so if they play a bad shot you think 'Well, I know it was a terrible shot but he can play better than that'. Possibly when I was captain it was the same. I picked Rose and Marks against the West Indies. Maybe they would not have been selected if someone else had been in charge.

For some reason there was a bit of tension between Mike Gatting and myself for several seasons. I suppose we emerged at the same time as Great White Hopes. We were rivals for the throne of English cricket. In New Zealand he was overshadowed and ever since then he has been rather intimidated by me – or so I'm told. We are similar characters, sergeant-major types, great competitors, only I'm more forceful than him, more belligerent. When I had my winter's rest in 1985, he was able to prove himself a fine Test cricketer; he'd always seemed so full of doubt before, exhibiting none of the bouncing pugnacity he showed with Middlesex. With England he tried to play differently, as if he was afraid that in five-day games you had to keep your left elbow up more than in three-day ones. With me out of the way he succeeded in his own manner in India and since then we've been able to do well together without Mike being forced into an unsuitable role. He is more certain of himself now that his Test career is well established, and in his new role as captain.

It was on that first trip to New Zealand that I established myself in Test cricket. Despite my troubles since I have never been dropped, other than as a result of disciplinary action. To be honest there hasn't been an all-rounder available to England who could match me even on a bad day. A few were tried – Chris Cowdrey, Ian Greig, Derek Pringle, Richard Ellison, Trevor Jesty – but none of them are genuine all-rounders in the sense that they could be selected as either batsman or bowler.

I ended the series in New Zealand with 212 runs and 17 wickets and played a big part in our Test victory. Also I had my first fights with Richard Hadlee. He was their main player, he still is, and he wanted to put down this upstart. I took him on, not believing in ducking challenges. He bounced me out for 19 in the second innings in the game we lost; I was caught hooking, looking terrible. Experience triumphs over wild youth, Somerset kid put in his place, all that stuff. Next Test I waited for him. He bounced me lots of times while he was fresh and I ignored them, waiting for him to tire. For some reason – it may have been the smile on my face – this angered him and he didn't bowl so well after that. I ended up with 133 in total and we won.

Several years after that tied series I was back there, in 1984.

We lost the series this time. My life changed enormously in those seven years, so much happened in a hell of a short time. I used to go out a lot more, with Bob Willis and J. K. Lever usually. I had so much energy. In fact I was out most of the time, joining in anything that was going, golf or whatever. But in 1984 I went out very little. You see, on the earlier tour, I could go out without being recognized; if anyone was pestered it would be Willis, not Lever or me. Now I was a marked man. Everywhere I went people would be pointing at me. I don't think I went to one nightclub. I went to cinemas a lot. I go to even more nowadays. I can sit down and once it gets dark I know I'm safe. It's crazy that, isn't it? Crazy.

Occasionally I'd visit some friends, go to a mate's house to listen to music or to water-ski or to talk. I'd avoid the main beaches. If the team were going for a trip on a yacht, I'd try to find a friend to go on a smaller yacht, just the two of us. I didn't want to be surrounded by the press – that wouldn't be a day off for me. I passed many days in my bedroom lounging around, using room service for food, avoiding people, listening to music. Music became a more important part of my life. You can't avoid retreating like this when you are recognized wherever you go.

In 1978 everything was new. Being on the other side of the world was a great adventure. I'd wake up and wonder what there was to do. In 1986 I prefer to go off in a silly hat and a pair of sunglasses hoping not to be recognized. As my career continues my lifestyle becomes more confined. I'd rather do my own thing than run with the pack. There are eyes everywhere.

I'm cut off from my Yeovil days, my Lord's groundstaff days, even my early Somerset days. I love to see old friends from those times but there's no point in pretending I can still muck in and be one of the lads. My mates understand this, they realize I have to be careful, living as I do in a greenhouse.

In my early days I was a bachelor, I didn't have much money

18

and what I had I spent: in debt to everyone, no plans, I'd live hand to mouth and see what fun the next day would bring. Now I have a tighter net of real friends who help me, not such a changing group of partners in crime.

In New Zealand I spent some time travelling around with Elton John and his band. I enjoyed that time more than any other on any tour anywhere. It was a closed environment. Hidden. I was accepted for myself, not for what I was. I could shut off totally, and forget about the rest of the world. With Elton's band I could mix in, and we could do crazy things in our own world where no one cared. Or we could sit and talk. Elton is very interested in sport, especially football. Suddenly, instead of getting drunk at the bar through boredom, I'd sit for hours simply chatting.

We talked about how our lives had changed, too. Reg Dwight's life has changed as much, if not more, than Ian Botham's.

Six or seven years ago I could go into a pub for a pint and a laugh with the lads. Now people watch me all the time, they stand off. People I've known for years do this and I don't feel relaxed and you can see they don't either. One evening recently Viv Richards, Andy Withers and I went to a club for a drink with some of Viv's friends. Where we stood there was a little circle, like a no-go area. The nightclub was crowded and yet there was this space around us, as if there was a force-field. When people did pass by, though, they wanted to bump into us, touch us – particularly some of the local toughies who wanted to show us they weren't impressed. What a strange situation.

People don't realize how important my fishing trips to Scotland are. I've been going there for ten years. It took me eight years to catch my first salmon but still I went back. I suppose people imagined that if I didn't catch one on the first day I'd throw away the rod and say it was a bloody silly sport. Far from it. My interest grew in the salmon when I learnt it was the hardest fish to catch, and now I understand the fish and what it does as well as anyone. The salmon is unpredictable – you have to outwit it. It's not one of these stupid fish a five-year-old could catch with a worm, it's a challenge.

I can go out on my own by the river and maybe not see another person all day. Allan Lamb enjoys that too – it's a different world up there, like being on Mars. In the evening we go to a pub where we've been going for eleven years and where I stay when I'm on my own. I'm Ian Botham the person, not Ian Botham the fellow who is in the headlines every other day. I'm just another fellow who comes salmon fishing. I fish from first thing in the morning, come rain or shine, till about five o'clock. I just stand there in the water – cold water it is up there too – till dusk. No food, nothing. Mind you, I make up for that in the evening, when I go back, have a hot bath and join the lads in the bar.

For the same reason I live three hundred miles from Taunton, two hundred and fifty miles from London. Epworth is a great place for me. There are two thousand people in the village. Everyone knows everyone, or just about; I have my local pub, Queen's, and I play football for them on Sunday. I'm just part of the village and that's how I want it. I go in, whether to butcher or baker, and everyone is just a good mate and we have a laugh. I come home some evenings and, say, they've had a young farmers' do and I've given an autographed bat to raffle, a week later I'll find a wheelbarrow full of peas or Brussels sprouts by my door. I lead a normal village life and if the press come looking for me, people will say 'Oh we haven't seen him in ages – don't know where he is.' I might be in the back room playing snooker. It is the same in Scotland. The press often appear there, hoping for a photograph of Botham fishing. The last thing I want to see is a camera. The people in Callandar will send them off on a wild-goose chase up the wrong river. They protect me.

Once, at home, a journalist simply walked through my front

door to try to interview me. I was with my wife in the back garden. Another time, when I was supposed to be overweight, they went around the shops in Epworth trying to find out what I ate! They even asked Liam – he was four at the time. If you are famous, there is nothing to stop reporters treating you and your family like that. It is much more difficult to be famous these days. Years ago a hero was taken as he presented himself. There wasn't much difference between a fellow in *Tiger* and Denis Compton, between Popeye and W. G. Grace. Now everything about you is described, everything investigated unsympathetically by people searching for a fresh angle to help sell their newspapers. It's shameful really, this creepy hunting for facts, selected facts, misleading facts. Have *you* nothing to hide? Never done anything wrong? If you're famous you have to be a saint or a sinner, you can't be a bloke who is, in some ways, like any other bloke. Imagine asking my infant son what I ate for lunch!

Your motivation changes as time goes on: the things you want from the game change. First of all your ambition is to get into the side and do well. Then as you establish yourself, you start to think about what you can make out of the game, and how you can develop your life. The Test before my first, they were paid £250 each and a London businessman came in because of Packer and suddenly it was £1,000. You do change, and instead of having three pints of bitter you might fancy a bottle of red wine instead.

I was reading recently about the footballer, Jim Baxter. He was saying that he had a whale of a time in soccer. He'd go to bed at 7.30 a.m., get up a few hours later and play a great role in a cup final. He gave parties, he gambled and so on but, in the end, it took its toll. That will never happen to me. It could have happened a few years ago when I lived for the moment, but I'm more conscious of what is going on now, I've grown up. I never want to grow up totally. I don't envy those blokes wandering round in suits and bowler hats because they look terribly bored. I'd rather go around in my jeans and leather jacket and feel happy. I have slowed down because I have commitments – a wife, children, a mortgage. I do believe tomorrow will take care of itself – you can't ruin your life by worrying about tomorrow. Let it take care of itself. I'm not like Jim Baxter.

It is tempting to abuse your fame. Your life brings you so much, and you could have an incredible time if you said yes to everything. These days I try not to go too far. I do have a bit of a break. You see, after a day's cricket you feel so excited you can't just have a shower and start examining your stamp album. The adrenalin is pumping too much. This is where the gambling and the drinking and the nightclubs come in to it. You feel it's something you've earned. I have late nights during Test matches very often. I won't go to bed till midnight; there's no point. As Joel Garner says, six good hours are better than nine hours of tossing and turning, reliving the day. I enjoy the merry-go-round of the Test lifestyle. If I have a day off I can sleep all the time, but when the adrenalin is flowing I try to unwind slowly – change, linger in the dressing-room for hours, a drink at the ground and then, if we're in the north where the beer is good, a pint or two at a pub with some of the lads. Then I'll drift off home.

I don't eat much in the evenings. One good meal a day will do me. That's another thing that has changed because I used to stuff myself all day long. Now I tend to eat more fish or chicken instead of wolfing down huge T-bone steaks three at a time. I rarely go to a nightclub these days, even on tour.

CHAPTER TWO

If It Hadn't Been For Cricket

Botham and I first met about sixteen years ago. We played in the Somerset Under-15s, with Dredge, Jennings, Slocombe and Marks, all county players. I can't remember much about him, though rummaging through scrapbooks I see that Bill Andrews regarded him as a 'very promising right-handed bat who has a lot of strokes'. A rare man, Bill, a man who sold wicket-keeping gloves to off-spinners. He was in charge of Somerset Under-19 cricket. Sometimes he seemed to find himself with no games for a while then three in one day, so he'd choose thirty-three players; but his division not being as good as his addition, it was rare for his teams to have quite the right number of players.

Bill did not mention Botham's bowling. He didn't bowl much in those days, certainly not as much as he wanted to. We regarded him as a bold hitter who would roll down a few off-breaks if anyone let him. Apparently he bowled seamers too, but we thought him too raw to try these in company. He could hit the ball though. Those scrapbooks, which cannot lie, reveal that Ian and I added 82 in one game of which my share was 15 (I was rather more aggressive in those days). I can't remember much about this partnership. Was it a wet day? I think it was. I think I remember some of Ian's hits. Certainly I can recall his brash character. I took to him, sensing a warmth beneath that reckless vigour.

This apparent refusal by others to take his bowling seriously

23

annoyed Ian. It was the same when he went to Liverpool for his England Schools trial. Vic Marks and I had already been selected to represent Hubert Doggart's Public Schools XI and Botham was fighting for a place in the ESCA team. He did reasonably well in the trials but was not chosen. His father says the selectors could not see the quality of his bowling. Probably this is accurate, but Botham could have upset them with his attitude too, which might not have been quite what was expected of a fifteen-year-old seeking to represent his country. In any event Botham was not taken seriously and he was rejected. Despite his wild conduct he has always wanted to be taken seriously. His most bitter, most lasting argument at Somerset was with a fellow young cricketer who (not without provocation) called Botham 'ignorant'. Botham had been cavorting around in the dressing-room in a manner designed to appeal to connoisseurs of the music-hall but not of the ballet. He never forgave his team-mate, for he had touched a sensitive nerve.

Ian says that without cricket he might have ended up 'inside'. This hints at a reckless, at times violent, side to his character. At school he was a member of a gang who would terrorize other kids. From school he went to the Lord's groundstaff where this aggression was appreciated. He went to Lord's because he could not very well stay at school, not being a serious student (he'd deliberately failed his eleven-plus because they played soccer at the secondary modern, rugby at the grammar school) and Somerset could not afford to employ him. He says he learnt discipline at Lord's from other groundstaff boys, though no one there seems to remember anything about that. At that stage he was still not a proper cricketer, and very few people thought he would succeed in county cricket. At sixteen years of age no one I know predicted that Botham would break through. We were certain Marks, Slocombe and Roebuck would. But Botham? Well, he might be a useful belter down the order but you couldn't play that way in county cricket – not against those fellows who could land the ball on a threepenny bit. No, he probably wouldn't amount to much. Two years later he was on the verge of international cricket.

Ian's irritation at not being allowed to bowl was symptomatic of his confidence. In 1974 Somerset (who realized that they could not afford *not* to employ Botham) signed Richards, Botham, Marks and myself. At once Botham informed Vic and me that he wanted all three of us to play for England together, the cricketing musketeers. That year he made his championship debut and cracked three boundaries before tamely lifting a catch to short cover. Storming back to the pavilion his regret was not that he had hit the ball in the air but that he hadn't struck the bloody thing higher. That was the last time he would ever lose his wicket in such a ruddy feeble way, or so he told everyone.

In 1976 Ian demanded his cap, threatening all sorts of things if he did not get his way. The committee bowed to his ambitions, realizing it seems that he had the power to demand. Those early years were full of spitting teeth (in one of Botham's first matches he was hit in the mouth as he hooked a bouncer from Roberts – he spat out a couple of teeth and 'one of the lads brought me a glass of water'); rows with Brian Close; huge sixes; and wickets taken with extraordinary deliveries. He was a handful to play with and against. In every game he contributed something spectacular. He would be brilliant or appalling, and pretty soon Somerset learnt to rely upon his spirit. Botham enjoyed those early intrepid years best of all. Climbing a mountain is a challenge, but what do you do when you get to the top? Some of us are still climbing, never perhaps to reach the summit. But the climb disciplines us.

In his first few seasons in cricket Botham was an overwhelming force, a magnificently competitive cricketer. He was honest, not merely in the matter of 'walking' and all that, but with his team and with himself. He wanted to be at the centre of things, he wanted to be dramatic and so he never held back, never feared failure. County cricket was not yet a prosaic experience. But he has not always been so excited by the game since. His belligerent fight back against Australia in 1981 was unusual in that it was provoked by peculiar circumstances: his loss of the captaincy sharpened his wits. Tennis players, notably Borg and McEnroe, can lose their edge in their mid-twenties. They play all year round too, and it is bound to take a toll.

In 1985, Botham's prodigious powers returned after a winter spent playing football, first in Scunthorpe and then in Yeovil. (He had been given a free transfer but boasts that he is now a double international, having captained England's non-league team.) Throughout May he performed heroics for his team, scoring 875 runs in the first 677 balls he faced in first-class cricket. Besides that his fielding was electrifying and his bowling faster than for years. He did not swing the ball quite so much, and could not be regarded as quite so lethal a threat as in 1978 but, overall, his cricket had returned to its greatest glory. Certainly his batting had discovered an authority, a majesty of stroke, since Botham, always a powerful back-foot player, had become a superb driver and puller. His game, rested for six months after eight years on the road, had been refreshed.

If he wanted to leave the game with his reputation unspoilt, Botham ought to have retired in 1981. As it is he carries on, still a mighty force and on the biggest of stages. If he is bored it is partly because too much is asked of him and partly the *hubris* which can set in when a star tires of his fame and the sacrifices which must be made to sustain it. In a sense, Botham's trouble is that he found the end of the rainbow too early in his life.

Ian's Story

My first memory is as a six-year-old, going out in the car with my father, my bat in the boot. We'd go to a game and I'd play for whichever team was short. I played with men right from the start, which taught me to hit the ball hard. In those games you couldn't sit on the splice with a pretty left elbow, you had to hit the ball.

I wasn't coached at home. Most cricketers I know are taught the basics by their dads in the back garden. I didn't have the patience for that. With me it wasn't a matter of learning things but of releasing me from my cage. I've always known how to play the shots, it's instinctive with me and I find movements easy to master. Obviously it helps to be a natural striker of the ball, with a good clean swing. Last summer I hit a golf ball on to a green at The Belfry, a green which had been reached previously by only Seve Ballesteros and Greg Norman. I can hit any ball a very long way, though I'm afraid I hit as many sixes at golf as I do at cricket! Most people restrict their swing whereas I pick up the bat very high and prepare to lace into the ball. Lads are taught to play their shots with care and with accuracy. I'm never bothered with that; I never read any of those coaching books which clutter your brain with detail.

I've only had about six hours of coaching in my career. They even gave up coaching me when I was at Lord's. It was the old story. They would ask me where my feet were and I would ask them if they had found the ball yet. There wasn't much anyone could do. Coaches rely upon a fellow being aware of his faults. I've never worried about that, because I've never tried to play perfectly. Some cricketers try to master a technique, so that every muscle in their body is absolutely under control. That isn't my way. They are like classical pianists who spend hours every day practising, whereas I'm like a jazz saxophonist who has a pretty good technique and wants to go into orbit . . .

As a youngster I was wild, very hard to control. It never occurred to me to worry about the future. If I could play soccer and cricket and go around with my mates that was all I asked. At junior school I was an outstanding cricketer, and so naturally the teachers coached the weaker players. They let me get on with my game. If I scored less than 50 I was disappointed. At school 25 was considered a good score and sometimes I'd reach my century. I stood ahead, sometimes a long way ahead. Lots of other kids probably did the same in other areas, but I didn't know anything about them. I think I had this arrogance, confidence and independence right from the start. I could hit sixes beyond anyone else's, which helped a lot. I am blessed with immense strength. I cannot explain why, because no one else in my family is particularly powerful. They are good sportsmen but nothing unusual.

I don't think my reluctance to listen to anyone did me any harm, though. I was a terrible bloke to try to coach because I was stubborn, but the people in charge could see that I wanted the team to do well and that I was improving. Anyway cricket wasn't a game our PE teachers enjoyed.

The only people I've ever really listened to are Ken Barrington and Vivian Richards. Viv helped me when I was struggling. He told me: 'You're the best. You know it, the world knows it, so believe it.' He was magnificent. I've never forgotten that. He still helps me if my game goes flat. Even I need a little bit of support occasionally. Viv will say that the darkest hour is just before the dawn, and I know he is right.

Tom Cartwright helped my bowling and I was sorry when he left Somerset, but the most help came from Ken Barrington. We spent hours together discussing everything. He was a lovely fellow, a real cockney without a bit of harm in him. He used to worry a lot, I think, though he kept this from us. Apparently he used to get in a terrible state because he was convinced that Charlie Griffith was a chucker. I saw Ken bat a few times and marvelled at his ability to get right behind the ball. He was like the rock of Gibraltar, a really patriotic, totally unbending cricketer. He was immensely proud of his country.

Besides these qualities Ken was a shrewd coach. It was all done in the nicest possible way. He'd tell me why I was getting out lbw, how to play short bowling, and slowly he lifted my game. He helped Gooch too, spending hours and hours in the nets with him. He was a fascinating man, a really unpretentious fellow, and he didn't go on about the past all the time. That was why I loved him.

People often talk as if there aren't any cricketers worth watching now. If you ever get a chance, have a look at a film of cricket in the 1960s. I watched one during a rain break in a Test. We had the radio on too, which is rare. Trueman was bowling, an old black and white film it was, and he was bowling medium-pace. On the radio Fred said, 'Isn't it funny how those black and white films make you look slower?' Ken would never have said that. He saw things as they were. People tend to remember all the good things about the past, none of the bad. Sometimes it seems as if cheating, bouncers, parties, England collapses, dropped catches and cursing were invented in 1974.

I used to play golf with Ken on tour and we'd talk things over then. He said wickets were so much better in his day because groundsmen had weeks, not days, to prepare them, since there were far fewer games. He said that bowlers are much faster now, with the odd exception like Frank Tyson. He said Trueman wasn't that quick, about my pace when I'm bending my back. Barrington believed that fielding is sharper and the game harder. People give away less. He watched Bradman's 300 at Leeds and at 250 they still had a silly mid-off and a silly mid-on. If a ball went two yards wide of a man he would shove out a boot and if he missed it he would amble off to fetch it. It's a different game now but people won't accept it. It's a faster game – just like soccer. Trueman would still be a good bowler, but he wouldn't be called Fiery Fred!

Tom Cartwright helped me too, though I think he tried to shape me more than Ken did. He wanted me to bowl in his style. Ken never wanted me to be defensive . . . but Tom did give me confidence. No one bowled me in the Under-15 unless

I forced them to. Cartwright wanted me to bowl in top-class cricket. For a time I tried to copy him (medium-paced swing, lots of patience). Then I realized it wasn't in my nature, that I would not be happy bowling 20–10–17–1. I'd rather get 5 for 100 in 20 overs, because you win games that way. Defensive bowling didn't suit my temperament. I've never been a patient bloke. Cartwright used to win games as well but his way took longer than mine. It was a matter of temperament. I could never have changed; it would have damaged my game. It's the way I am, that's all. It was the same at school: I was aggressive, I wanted to do things now, not tomorrow. I was in trouble all the time. If it hadn't been for cricket I'd have ended up inside. I've often said that.

It's a pity cricket is played all year round, though. I'd be far more sane and maybe better and more consistent if I had winters off. Sometimes I'm jaded even before we go away. In cricket you do it alone. You are on the stage as an individual. It's you against them. And although you enjoy both aspects, the team and the individual, you are under constant pressure. That's why I enjoy soccer so much – there's no pressure, because I'm just an ordinary bloke in the team.

From Lord's I went to Somerset in 1974. We were on £15 a week and we worked the scoreboard. We were cheap and so it didn't matter if we did well or not. Now youngsters are better paid and under more pressure. I suppose I made an impression because there were few eighteen-year-olds around in those days. There are far more teenagers now because the game is so athletic. A lot more is expected too. Our senior players could have been our fathers – Close, Parks, Cartwright . . . even Derek Taylor!

I had to battle because I was young – people kept saying I was *too* young and it was infuriating. Last August we chose Jonathan Atkinson to play for Somerset. He's still at school and, since he had barely turned seventeen, several people said he was too young. You're never too young if you are good enough. Boris Becker didn't think he was too young, and neither did Atkinson. He scored 79 and we added nearly 200.

Cricket used to be regarded as a craft you had to learn. You were supposed to serve an apprenticeship during which the master craftsmen helped you and protected you. Our modern game is more immediate – it isn't only a matter of skill, it is also a question of vigour, agility, strength and ambition, qualities found in youngsters. Craftsmen are getting left behind because they are too slow, because people do not merely want to study technique, they want to watch a drama.

My own rise was swift because there were few all-rounders at the time. Greig went to Packer, Old was injured as usual and, out of the blue, they had to blood me. Suddenly I was England's all-rounder. Two years before people laughed when I said I could bowl. My sudden ascendancy surprised everyone – well, nearly everyone! It's hard to say why it happened. It's not as if I was a child prodigy; remember, I was never chosen for English Schools. But I did want to do well, shamelessly, and I was arrogant. On that first trip to New Zealand I had to make runs in the opening game. It was do or die. I willed myself to a century. I wanted it so badly. My career depended upon it. I am extremely wilful, which may be a fault, but it has certainly helped my cricket. I just don't listen to what other people say, and I just don't care what I look like. I don't care if people are impressed or not. I don't worry about making a fool of myself, I don't play safe, not in any part of my life. This has led me into scrapes, but they are only the other side of the coin. People who enjoy watching swashbuckling sixes can't really complain if the swashbuckler swashbuckles in pubs too!

From the start of my career I would never retreat. Even in my first Test in 1977 the Australians tried to treat me with contempt. I wasn't worried when I began badly. I didn't care if people said my 5 wickets were a fluke. Anyway, how can 5 wickets be a fluke? I had them, and I was going to get 5 more tomorrow, and if not tomorrow the day after. In my second Test I took 5 for 20 and no one could argue with that.

Also I loved Test matches from the start. Some people are too shy to play in the vast arena with every ball covered by every paper, and on radio and television. Your faults are exposed and reported and unless you are an extrovert these things can dig deep into your confidence. Some players at Somerset were not suited to cup finals, they didn't enjoy the feeling of being in the big smoke, and were much better players at home, among their own. I am the opposite. I love Test cricket. From the start I knew it was for me. I liked the crowds, the atmosphere, the noise, the excitement, everything. I still get this buzz as soon as I walk on to the ground for the first day's play.

An overwhelming sense of drama hits you. You can see it on people's faces. You arrive at the ground and you know it is a Test match. It is your country against theirs and for one day you live in a world entirely cut off from everything else. In the evening you watch the highlights on television. I like Richie Benaud because he is sharp, but tries not to do down the players. In the morning you read your *Sun* and see your game of cricket described in blazing headlines. Maybe there are people in England who do not know the score. If there are, you never meet any of them.

There was one tour in India when the Tests were boring. We lost the first, which is disastrous over there. After that you couldn't get anyone out. We tried like hell for two days but still at the end of the second day India would be 400 for 4 and you would realize that was the end of the game. It was hard work. Apart from that I've loved every day of my Test career.

CHAPTER THREE

It Sort Of Clicks

Botham suggested that I talk to Michael Brearley. We found ourselves playing in a benefit game for Ian in London (Botham's benefit was not so much a Somerset collection as a national appeal) and after lunch we sat down for a chat. In the meantime Botham was batting, facing county bowling on a damp pitch. A transcript of our conversation follows: it is included because I feel that it gives such an apt picture of the man we were discussing, interspersed as it is with our astonished comments on the huge hits which erupted into the car park (Brearley feared for his vehicle). Moreover, as he drifted towards recklessness, having satisfied the sponsors, Botham tried a few irregular blows, each one succeeding however difficult the hand and eye coordination required. Radio One disc-jockey Andy Peebles is the announcer.

Roebuck: 'Botham wasn't too pleased when you said Old could bat better than him.'
Brearley: 'I didn't know Botham well. I'd seen him in a county game and he appeared raw – powerful but raw. In the nets in Pakistan he couldn't lay a bat on the local leg-spinners. He didn't look much good.'
Roebuck: 'Why did you go along with this Guy the Gorilla rubbish? I was disappointed with you . . . I'd thought it was obvious that there was more to him than that, obvious that he *wanted* to be taken for an oaf.'

Brearley: 'I was hostile at first . . . you knew him well . . . in Pakistan we wondered why we'd brought him. He was brash and played like a cheerful, wild hitter from club cricket.'
Roebuck: 'So why did you change your mind?'
Brearley: 'He played terrifically well in New Zealand under Boycott. He showed a lot of guts in his battles with Hadlee and he bowled his heart out. Also he deliberately ran Boycott out because he was scoring too slowly. That endeared him to everyone.'
(Peebles: 'Ladies and gentlemen, that's Ian Botham's century.')
Brearley: 'I don't know how you survive in this environment.'
Roebuck: 'I barely do. Why has Botham achieved so much?'
Brearley: 'He has an extraordinary ability . . . look at that shot . . . he isn't just an ordinary boy from Yeovil. He is phenomenally strong. He hits the ball twice as hard as anyone else . . .'
Roebuck: 'Has his success . . . that's a fantastic shot! That's six!'
Brearley: 'It was outrageous.'
Roebuck: 'A left-handed hook for six. Can you do that?'
Brearley: 'No.'
Roebuck: 'He has an inner belief . . . you can see it when he succeeds. He likes to be nonchalant. A moment of joy escapes but he tries to show that it was natural. It's an expression of arrogance.'
Brearley: 'Look at that . . . near my car! You can't say that is ordinary batting. He's *not* an ordinary boy from Yeovil. He has staggering ability.'
Roebuck: 'You couldn't have seen that at fifteen or seventeen. No one I've met has said they knew he would be a cricketer of brilliance. Look at the height of that one! He's not outstanding at anything else . . . Why Botham? Why not someone else?'
Brearley: 'He didn't stop. He isn't afraid. He explores his limits. He plays in Test matches as if he were in a club game.'
Roebuck: 'This is courage, isn't it? The courage to find out how

good you are. Most of us want to live within a harbour, Botham is in the raging seas.'

Brearley: 'Look at that! It's staggering. He is brave – but it works because he's bloody good. He has a reckless, shameless determination.'

Roebuck: 'Out! What's that, 132?'

(Peebles: 'Ladies and gentlemen, a round of applause for Ian Botham.')

Brearley: 'Extraordinary. It was an extraordinary innings in a benefit game in London in September. No one else can bat like that.'

Roebuck: 'In that series against Australia . . . he says his luck was bound to turn.'

Brearley: Maybe. Could be I owe him more than he owes me I suppose. He thinks it was all coincidence?'

Roebuck: 'Yes. The wheel of fortune. He's played well for Somerset as captain.'

Brearley: 'He needed an adviser, especially after Barrington died. Who was there to listen to? Viv was not around and no one else was really on his level. If I did anything it was to restore his confidence, to release him from trying too hard and playing too tentatively.'

Roebuck: 'He wants to be captain again. He wants to win people's respect. I think he wants to be taken a bit more seriously. Towards the end of their careers sportsmen often start thinking about posterity. Particularly if he wants to captain England.'

Brearley: 'I doubt if he'll get it again. You don't often get a second chance as England captain.'

Roebuck: 'It is dear to his heart.'

Brearley: 'What would he do to get it?'

Roebuck: 'Quite a lot. Do you find him ruthless?'

Brearley: 'He adapts well to company. With me he is the wild child, but I've seen him as a hard-headed businessman too. I've learnt not to underestimate him.'

35

(Ian Botham comes into the pavilion)
Roebuck: 'Well played, Ian.'
Brearley: 'Well done.'
Ian: 'Cheers, lads.'

There we were, two Cambridge graduates, trying to define Botham's peculiar talent, while in front of us he gave ample evidence of it. At the very moment that I was trying to extract from Brearley some piercing insight into how this hefty Yeovil boy had developed into so prodigious a cricketer, Botham's left-handed hook flew over point's head and bounced a yard inside the boundary, amazing us both. Seeing such shots, we could not avoid the conclusion that here was an extraordinarily gifted man at his work.

Oddly, Botham was at his most joyous in that game. I do not know why. He had been on breakfast television that morning and had been strangely rude to his host, showing to the public all those loud-mouthed failings for which he is so roundly criticized. Yet he batted in a cheerful, inspiring manner, giving of his best to his audience.

It is not easy for a brilliant games-player to define his gift. Why was Greaves in that place at that time? What was he doing there? Why did Best go round the full-back that way? Why did Piggott choose that particular gap, that particular moment to drive a horse for home? So much of sport is instinctive. A chess player can explain his moves, whereas a cricketer will shrug his shoulders and say that he was just following an idea he had. Perhaps this is why a lot of sportsmen gamble and drink; they learn to rely upon their nerve, upon instincts which they cannot define. Perhaps, too, this is why sporting heroes so often appear incoherent. How do you define a gift? Could Ludwig von Beethoven explain why he began his Fifth Symphony in that abrupt manner? Where did the notes come from? Why had no one else thought of them?

Botham could not shed much light upon his genius, beyond

saying that it is a sixth sense, that something 'sort of clicks'. He remembered catching Gomes off Ellison in 1984, and recalled that he had not been aware of the catch. The ball had ended up in his hands and he had been forced to watch the highlights to see what had happened. In one of his first games for Somerset – against Pakistan at Bath in 1974 – he was fielding at long-off. Asif Iqbal hit a lofted off-drive. At once Botham charged in and, diving, he took the ball low and at full stretch. It was a remarkable catch physically, but the point here is that there was no calculation, he ran after it at once. This may be a part of his gift, this ability to let the instinct take over without listening to the cautions advanced by reason: his immediate realization of where the ball is and his simultaneous charge after it. It is as if Botham can abandon himself completely to the game, as if he were a part of it rather than someone trying to play it. Piggott riding, Boycott batting – each has a quality of absorption, so that he appears not to concentrate because he is already totally single-minded. Botham exhibits this quality too, this absolute surrender of himself to what he is doing.

We decided to rake over Botham's famous innings. He regarded the Headingley innings as hilarious and the Old Trafford effort as far more substantial in that it was carefully constructed. At Headingley, Dilley and Botham swung lustily and enjoyed themselves. But Ian observed that only Richards or himself, possibly one or two others, could have played such an innings. He says that Boycott restrains himself, as do most of us, leaving his aggression behind in the nets.

Few cricketers are prepared to take as many chances as Botham, because failure is a terrible thing. He, every time he bats or bowls, gives himself the chance to succeed gloriously and, of course, to fail dreadfully. Every time he bats he tries to demolish the bowling; every time he bowls he seeks to shatter the stumps. This is not so with other cricketers. Few dare to explore their talents for the hell of seeing how far they go. Botham is a cricketing anarchist, he respects no rule, bows to no circumstance. To a team he offers hope – until he is finished the game is not lost – but sometimes his maverick spirit, his jovial destruction of order leads his team to rely too much upon sweat and inspiration. (Usually Botham's sweat and inspiration.)

Perhaps Brearley is correct in his suggestion that Botham has succeeded because he did not stop where others stopped, he treated Test matches as if they were club games. If so, it explains also the hostility towards Botham felt by many old cricketers, most of whom respect cricketing manners and techniques. It is significant that the stories upon which we were brought up included the ability of bowlers to land the ball on a threepenny bit, the way batsmen 'sniffed' the ball, didn't cut before June and kept their left elbows high. These stories impressed us, intimidated us even, as youngsters, and we were awed by the discipline and the craft of our profession. Botham had little patience with that. He just wanted to belt the ball and was prepared to do so come hell or high water.

Ian's Story

I've played three or four innings which I'll remember with pride, innings to tell my grand-children about if I live so long! I'll name them. One was in Sydney when I stayed in for ninety minutes and hit 6 runs. Another was for Somerset in a cup semi-final at Lord's: I scored 90 odd under pressure that day. And then there was the 1981 innings at Old Trafford, which was much better than the Headingley 100 the previous month. We were roaring with laughter at Headingley. The match was lost so we decided to have a go. We'd booked out of the hotel and my golf clubs were in the boot. It inspired a lot of people, the noise was demented, especially when Willis bowled Alderman to win the match. I watch that video sometimes and still it seems make-believe. When Dilley and I were in we laughed and joked, seeing who could play the most idiotic stroke. He

38

hit two booming drives off the side edge to the boundary, real Chinese cuts. He laughed and so did I. In the end it was *Boy's Own* stuff, it was going to happen and so there was no pressure. On reflection we felt like men in a play, following a script someone else had written. Everything had a dreamy feeling about it, particularly since it happened so quickly. It was like a mad interlude in a serious drama. For four days the batsmen had hardly been able to survive. Balls were lifting, cutting, shooting. You could be out at any moment. Suddenly, for two hours, we swiped and the score rattled up on the board. They were dazed, while we scarcely knew what we were doing. An air of unreality hung over it all. I batted like a maniac, being free to do so because our position was hopeless. It was a gambler's last throw. I suppose someone who isn't a gambler would not have dared so much, but more fool them. Angels would never have won that game for England.

I had no idea we were 100 in front when Dilley was out. We thought we were still behind. It was a confusing session! When we realized our position we knew we had a chance. It was a lethal pitch. The Aussies knew the ball was moving and jumping like a Harrier. We'd either missed the ball by a foot or edged it over the slips. That was the only difference between us and the other fellows. It was luck. On a bad wicket you must have lots of close fielders. If two blokes start swiping anything can happen: in an hour these men with their long handles can disrupt a team which has dominated a match. The Australians deserved to win, in effect they'd already won. Having the game stolen like that must have left them shattered. I was talking to Border when we watched the video this summer and he said they were quite happy for me to get 50 or 60 but suddenly they realized that Graham Dilley was doing the same. Border said they had lost control before they realized what was happening. They were thinking overnight that they might not get us out and they might have to get 200, and it preyed on them. They were beaten by the end of the fourth day. Brearley went into their dressing-room at the end of that day's play and they were sitting around in total silence.

But mine wasn't a great innings, it wasn't really an innings at all – just an almighty heave. I didn't put anything into it, I didn't walk out and say 'Right, we're in a mess, and I'm going to sort it out'. That's why Old Trafford was far superior. There I went out with the purpose of winning the game.

When you really bat, time has no meaning. You get caught up with it. Gavaskar will never look at the clock or the scoreboard. It's the same with driving sometimes – when you're driving well, you can travel a hundred miles and hardly remember a thing. That frightens some people but it shouldn't. When I'm doing well I go into this trance, whereas when I'm doing badly I'm thinking about my movements. You can be too . . . *present* at cricket, too aware of time and place. To do well you need to be like an actor who is utterly at one with his character. If he is standing there saying 'Now is the winter of our discontent' and wondering what's for tea, he won't be much good. You have to lose yourself in batting. If I'm laughing around it means that it is an innings on which it is wrong to place much value.

In a sense, my best innings was in a cup semi-final against Middlesex in 1983. It was a team innings, and I gave myself totally to it. We were 53 for 5 at one stage; Nigel Popplewell and Vic Marks stayed in and played really well. At tea-time I can remember just sitting there already exhausted. You can't bat like that every day, concentrating totally, head down, because it drains you, especially if you are a bowler and captain too. The scores were level in the last over and as we'd lost 4 wickets, I only had to block it out – only I didn't like this word 'only'. I've never felt so nervous in my life: one run to win and there I am blocking every ball! Once I was close to being lbw, very close. There were people all around me, Radley at silly point, someone else at short leg. It isn't natural for me to block and I'm not used to people staring at me from a yard away. They were safe, too! I dreaded every ball. Somehow we survived and I can remember charging from the field, a bit like when we won in 1981. Suddenly there is such a feeling of release and you can't stop yourself. You see it on video later and you realize you look an idiot. It's not very English, is it? Charging about, waving your bat in the air. But everyone was doing it in 1981 and 1983. I don't see what is wrong with it. The West Indians dance a jig every time they take a wicket. We are so formal, so stiff, and it shows in the way we bat. In 1981 and 1983 I felt like shouting and drinking, so I did.

People remember these famous innings, and imagine I'm the only fellow to play them. It's because I go in at six. If the opener plays a heroic innings no one notices because they say the pitch is good, and usually the later batsmen do well too as the bowlers tire. You get noticed at six, leading your team's fight back like Sobers. How many times did he save the West Indians? He was my hero, though he's been pretty rude about me. If he'd gone in at three or four he'd have scored as many runs but been noticed less. Batting at 35 for 2 is quite different from going in at 50 for 4. Six is a dramatic place to bat, the cornerstone of the eleven. Either you're a great hero or a bloody idiot. Your team is either 50 for 4 or 290 for 4. In both situations, to me attack is the best policy. Vic Marks has the same attitude at Somerset. There's no point in grafting if it is not your game. You can only do what you are good at.

I'll never play another innings like the one at Sydney, when I scored 6 in, oh, hours. It seemed hours anyway. I didn't enjoy it. I changed my game for the situation and that was a mistake. I'll never do it again, though I suppose I had no choice. I don't know if you remember the game – Randall scored 150 and we turned the tables on the Aussies to win the series. It was unbelievably hot; you felt you were toasting. Adelaide is usually the hottest place, with those northerly winds off the Nullarbor, but Sydney was hot that week – 45°C or something. I'd bowled twenty-eight overs because Willis and Hendrick

41

were suffering from heat exhaustion. They stood under cold showers and were sick. Hyperventilation or something, or drinking lots of water. Maybe it was the 'goo' which saw me through. Water's useless unless there's some whisky in it.

I was told to stay in. It was vital. It was more a matter of time than runs. But I went too far. I was out to a long hop or a full-toss or something. I hardly realized what had happened. I'd sunk into such a defensive frame of mind that I saw this bad ball and chipped it to mid-wicket – incredibly frustrating. I've never played like that since.

I see cricket as entertainment, on a stage. You have to stay true to yourself, irrespective of everything. Next time there might be two or three blokes with scarlet fever in our dressing-room and I'll go for my shots just the same. I've learnt never to restrain myself, never to be cowardly. Sydney was the only time I forgot. We won the game, but I'll never do it again. Drinking milk isn't my game either.

People often ask me about particular innings, some of Viv's (especially that 153 in Melbourne) and some of mine. They ask if they can be explained; I don't think so. Nothing feels different before you go in. You are just the same old fellow. It just happens. It sort of clicks. We have a chance of these things because we have no inhibitions, no pattern. We don't apply a formula, as if we were knitting a jumper. We're more like those modern artists who throw tons of paint on the canvas. We just want to hit the ball as hard and as often as possible. Nothing is held back. Blokes like Boycott restrain themselves: they're always thinking 'Don't get out, don't do anything silly', talking to themselves. They don't trust themselves and so they restrain their instincts. They see cricket as a discipline and conduct themselves as rigidly as soldiers. To me the game is a chance to see what you can do; I find all that defensive business very boring.

Batsmen like me are prepared to improvise and to react to a mood. It is the same with catches – Asif in Bath, Shepherd at Taunton in 1979, Mendis last year. I just see the ball and feel myself going for it. I'm not standing at slip instructing myself to stay down, or to watch the edge of the bat. My mind is empty and free, and I wait to see what happens. The Shepherd catch, for example – I didn't know where the ball was, I just ran. A sixth sense just took over. I can't explain it. I found myself in the right place, reached out my hands and there was the ball. Viv said the same when he caught me at Lord's in the 1979 World Cup final. He ran fifty yards and caught me at full stretch. I said, 'We needed 9 an over. You might have given me a break.' He said he hadn't thought he could possibly get there.

In 1984 I caught Larry Gomes off Ellison. The lads were all jumping up and down, shaking my hand, and there was the ball. I had to watch television to see what had happened. You cannot explain these things logically. Your mind is empty and something just explodes. I don't know why I can do these things when no one else even sees the ball. Certainly I stand close, but that's because I hate it when the ball falls in front of the slips. There's nothing more frustrating for a bowler. Maybe it's a bit of arrogance which enables me to catch these half-chances – because I have no doubts. And I leave my hands on my knees. Partly this *is* arrogance, partly simply tempting fate, and partly because it's a reasonable place to put them. You've no idea where the catch is coming from, it could be low, could be wide, could be straight. Might as well relax until you see it. Anyway, that's my story. Also, the more the old codgers criticize me for it, the more I do it. Things like that provoke old timers incredibly, far more than things which matter. It is strange, however rebellious a fellow was in his day, however free his spirit, as soon as he has a pen in his hand or a microphone in front of him he starts yapping about discipline. There are a lot of poachers turned gamekeepers around! Truth is, they did it their way and I do it my way. If they'd taken every criticism to heart they'd never have succeeded.

Batting is much the same I find. Viv and I never have a net when we are in form. We don't want to stop the flow. It's the same when people say it's tea-time or something. I start scratching about and then I lose my wicket. Suddenly your mind is full of irrelevant details. Instead of whacking the ball you start thinking about holding the fort till tea. I did that in Bath . . . I was going well and then Peter Roebuck said to be careful because Wayne Daniel was in his last over and we could get after the others. Daniel bowled a full toss and I was just moving into it when my brain went click, I tried to place the ball, and chipped it to mid-wicket. I should have clobbered the ruddy thing into the tents.

Sometimes I will myself to score runs, like Willis wills himself to catch a ball. When it's in the air you can see him begging God (or maybe it's Bob Dylan) to let him catch it. He steels himself, forces himself to take the catch. He hardly missed a chance in his Test career. Viv shows that same will power, especially in cup finals. He says to himself 'Viv must score a hundred'. Everyone else is hoping not to make a fool of themselves, but Viv will accept nothing less than a hundred. In 1982 when we bowled Nottinghamshire out for 130 he was furious . . . well, disappointed. He asked how he was going to score his hundred! It didn't occur to him that he'd fail. He was 51 not out when we won the game. He scored hundreds in 1979 in the World Cup and Gillette Cup finals and in 1981 against Surrey. Another time, when Roebuck and Popplewell were seeing us home against Kent he paced around on the balcony saying, 'Take me to Lord's, boys, take me to Lord's'. He couldn't stop himself. He wanted the great stage. It is pure will, for Willis and Richards, they simply tell themselves to do it right. They won't accept less from themselves.

Viv and I, our characters are a mixture of arrogance, confidence and belief. Ian Chappell and his cronies, they were pretending, acting tough. Chappell was a coward. He needed a crowd around him before he would say anything. He was sour like milk that had been sitting in the sun for a week. Viv and I are not afraid of failure, or of ourselves. Maybe that sounds like boasting. There are a dozen blokes who could be as good as us but they don't believe in themselves. It's a matter of courage, the same as it is with Boycott. He hides behind his batting average, which is usually pretty, and he uses it as an excuse to himself for playing so far within his abilities. He pretends he has little ability and is all application. That's rubbish. He's a brilliant cricketer, as anyone who saw him play one-day cricket in Australia will testify. He hides, he wants to be boosted by standing on top of the averages. Really great players are more arrogant than that.

CHAPTER FOUR

Ian and The
Railway Sleeper

In *Beyond a Boundary*, C. L. R. James's study of cricket intellectual snobbery, the author observes that batting twenty-five years ago was dull and conformist. He saw none of the courage and imagination which Trumper, Ranjitsinhji and Compton had brought to the game. He believed that cricketers had sunk into a 'welfare state of mind', arguing that daring, adventure and creativity had been succeeded by a desire for security from the professionals. It was not, for Mr James, a problem of technique but of philosophy of life. He said that MCC could appoint committees to investigate the drabness to which the game had been reduced but none of them would do any good. They could not change the 'dyed-in-the-wool' attitudes of the day. Mr James suggested that the only hope lay in the possibility that some young romantic might arrive to disturb the conservatives, as Grace and Ranjitsinhji had done, and to change current techniques. He 'will hit against the break so hard and so often that the poor bowlers will wish he would go back to hitting with it. He will drive overhead and push through any number of short legs, as W.G. used to do, so that a whole race of bowlers will go underground for fifteen years as they did once and once more emerge with a new bag of tricks. Our romantic will do these things . . . and the big battalions will follow.'

County cricketers are a cautious lot. Though they've scored runs throughout their careers they do not trust their luck.

They construct a technique in which imagination plays no part. Everything is tight, everything is predictable. Probably the captain is pleased, certainly the committee are. Indulgence in flights of fancy can bring grim results. A good cricketer is paid £8,000. If he scores 800 lovely runs they cost the club £10 each, if he contributes 1,600 runs the cost is down to £5 a run, or £20 for an edge over the slips. It is a matter of productivity. He learns some tricks of the trade, gathers wisdom from his failures and tries to churn out runs as reliably as a cow brings forth milk. Lots of cricketers began their careers with noticeable individuality. Even so dull a cricketer as Roebuck used to hook every bumper he received (he has been hit four times on the head but desisted because too often his wicket was lost). In his first championship innings he lifted the opening bowlers back over their heads. At school his late cut was as frequent as his leg drive (which has survived). But he is a worrier, uncertain of his merit. Too often in his younger days he lost his place in the team. Eventually he embarked upon a policy of resistance, not so much to draw the sting from the opposition as to cement his place in the eleven. Much may have been lost along the way, especially a little of that daredevil spirit which lies within, forever suppressed.

Such is the approach of the professional. It is cricket as a discipline, as a duel between tuned instruments. A county cricketer relies upon fear to conquer his natural wit. If it is not cricket of the welfare state it may be cricket of the baked bean.

Botham is not a part of this drift. His batting has not changed since he was at school. His headstrong character has given him certainty. He can be an astute, helpful observer of faults in friends and rivals. He has advised Boycott, and usually his comments are valuable. But he does not study his own game, he is not a fellow to ponder upon his left elbow or right thumb. Whereas Boycott, Gavaskar and Border – superb collectors of runs – are men dedicated to the mastering of the orthodox, Botham is a maverick. No one has batted as he does in Test cricket; who was the last man, let alone the last Englishman, to heave two of his first three deliveries for straight sixes? He has brought audacity back to the game.

Botham is a magnificent cutter, puller and defender. His drives are straight, and full of authority. He has a good technique and also he has the nerve to explore beyond it. His game is not subdued by fret. He hits the ball to funny places and loves to destroy a bowler's length. He forces the bowler to try something different. In doing this against the most brilliant bowlers, Botham exhibits a freedom from undue respect for craftsmanship and from unfair disrespect for violence. He lifts the ball over extra cover against the break. He sweeps back-handed in Test matches (though Mr May has frowned upon this). He can even hook back-handed. He can cut the fastest bowlers with a delicacy that surprises. He can withdraw from his stumps to angle the ball through point. He has been able to mix brutal power, imagination and nerve. Others have followed. Back-handed sweeps are not as rare as they were. Everyone now steps back from the stumps to counter the angles of defensive bowling. Lots of hitherto cautious batsmen use their feet to smite the 'step-and-fetch-it' bowlers (Botham's euphemism for spinners). In 1986 batsmen are not as concerned with the intricacies of orthodoxy. Lots of batsmen in the middle order give the ball a hefty crack, abandoning 'tip the forelock' discipline.

Botham has helped to bring spirit back to batting. Youngsters can give the ball a fearful clout and invoke Botham in their cause. Back-alley cricket has been brought to Lord's.

Botham is not alone in using a heavy bat. Clive Lloyd and Graham Gooch use them, as do lots of other top cricketers. Not all of them can handle such a blunderbuss with the efficiency of Botham – in his hands it is like an epée – and not everyone rejoices in the violence its use can bring to the game. Spinners complain that the contest is no longer fair. They used to float the ball into the air, inviting and hoping to defeat the strike.

They say now that edges from these meaty bats carry over cover and skid to the boundary. They say that to be economical they must dart the ball into the batsman's pads at an angle which restricts the full swing of the bat. They search for the inside edge, and flash the ball at the wickets rather than wide of them to a packed cover field. In ten years heavy bats have changed the battle between bowler and batsman. Cricket has lost some of its subtlety. However, it is still possible for a thirty-eight-year-old leg spinner to bamboozle the West Indians.

Botham has changed batting. He arrived as a cheerful bully cutting a swathe through the game, a Thatcherite scorning the prissiness of emancipated man. With his batting and with his personality (for good or ill) he has revitalized English cricket. He is not another cricketer of the welfare state, not a cricketer off the production line. He is not a batsman smothered by the statistics of the dull-witted. He has more Churchill in him than Beveridge. Whether it is worth it I cannot say (Ian and I take opposing views on almost everything) but he has certainly brightened things up . . .

Ian's Story

Sir Len Hutton came into the England dressing-room one day, picked up one of my bats and wrote in the paper that I used a railway sleeper! He suggested that it restricted my game, turning me into a hitter rather than a batsman with a variety of strokes. I've never found it so. In tennis players are using rackets with bigger heads, finding that this gives them more power and more spin. In other sports – golf for example – I imagine the manufacturers are searching for better clubs so that the players can hit the ball further. Any sportsman knows the difference good equipment makes. If your racket is no good you lose your touch. You're always having to hit the ball rather than letting the racket do the work for you. It's the same in cricket. If your bat is no good you have to give the ball some real beef. If it sounds beautiful, if you hear that meaty sound the poets write about, you do not need to swipe. I think Sir Len was wrong. I've found that using a heavy bat has given me the confidence to strike rather than to slog the ball: it has improved my game. I do not need to slash but can play controlled shots. I can late cut and sweep with the best of them. I played a late cut off Jeff Thomson last year and it positively flashed through the slips. That gave me a lot of satisfaction. Maybe tennis players feel prouder of a delicate little drop shot than of a blistering ace.

I enjoy trying new shots. This back-handed sweep – I'm not allowed to play it now in Test cricket because I missed one against Holland last summer – everyone says it is a crazy shot. Imagine how the bowler feels: his field is set, he is tying down the batsman, and he bowls a ball just where he wants it so that the batsman is bound to hit it towards his fieldsmen. Suddenly, this lunatic is playing left-handed and the ball is flying to the boundary! They hate it. Especially Underwood. He curses and growls. Where is he to bowl next? What ball can be delivered safely? The captain scratches his head. This idiot might do it again . . .

If I'd been caught at square leg no one would have minded. That was the obvious thing to do. But you have to surprise them, certainly in these limited-overs games. You have to hit the ball where there are no fieldsmen even if it is risky. There were six blokes on the leg side. I have been out back-sweeping a few times, and people have said I was irresponsible. I don't agree. Sometimes you can win a game with just one audacious shot. It destroys all the plans because plans are made with the idea that the batsman is predictable, or at least sane! At times like this it is only when I'm walking back that it occurs to me that some people will be displeased with my dismissal. I never think of that beforehand.

My bats are extremely heavy – I doubt if anyone else uses a heavier one, not even Graeme Pollock or Clive Lloyd. Graham

Gooch and I find that with a heavy bat and a high backlift we can hit through the line of the ball and even edges will fly away. Gooch often edges the ball to the square leg boundary. People say 'tremendous shot', but sometimes it's simply an edge which, with a light bat, would be dangerous.

We have influenced a lot of other cricketers by breaking a taboo. You hear that Bradman and Compton used feather-weight bats and writers argued that this helped their cutting and hooking. Hence they used to lecture us on avoiding bats that we could not manoeuvre. This is true with kids. You see some of them trying to learn the game with things that resemble tree trunks, which is terribly damaging. But Gooch and Richards and I are very strong men. We can hook and cut as well as anyone and heavy bats add thunder to our drives. Bowlers know that we use them – it's part of our mystique. As I walk out I can see them thinking, 'Hell, here's Botham with that bloody log'. It's a part of the way of beating them: I can use a bat like this and what are you going to do about it? In a way it gives you a swagger, a bit like being the fastest gun in the west. Mind you, everyone's at it now, or at least everyone with the strength. They all realize the advantage of weight. Bowlers are always chucking bouncers at you. It's nice to stand there with this ruddy great thing in your hands and give them something in return.

Another thing I do which I've noticed other people copying is hitting the ball over extra cover. This is an accepted method in one-day cricket because the bowlers aim at leg-stump and put their men on the leg boundary. Actually I've always tended to favour the off side. At school the ball would lift over mid-off, sometimes over point. My natural swing was inside out, rather like Lee Trevino. It isn't quite as obvious these days but even now my straight hits usually fly over long-off. I'm not so good at hitting the ball over long-on.

Australia realized this at Lord's in 1985. Allan Border put a man at deep backward point and I tried to drive Lawson over mid-off as he expected. The ball swung away and I was caught by Greg Ritchie in front of the Tavern. It wasn't a respectable way to lose your wicket in a Test match. On the other hand I am committed to attack and that is why opposing teams fear me. It is because I will continue to attack even if things are going wrong, even when sensible people are saying 'Oh come on, lad, get your head down'. I don't listen to these whispers. Sometimes my approach works and if it does we usually win. If it fails, well at least I was man enough not to be intimidated. Australia and other teams are afraid of such power and such recklessness. If I curtail these qualities they won't be nearly as worried. I've been given strength and a lot of ability – it is up to me to use them and to ignore those fellows who want me to be like everyone else. I don't regret being caught off Lawson. I don't regret anything. Every approach has its failings. Probably it's just as well I have a thick skin. So many people put you up against an ideal. So many people want me to play like Boycott and Boycott to play like me.

Apparently in 1985 I'd scored 870 runs off 695 balls at one stage. Others are batting in the same way. Despite what you read I'm convinced people score much faster these days. As I've said, our cricket is more aggressive. Batsmen play in a different way, not like a bunch of old grannies on a weekly outing.

I don't know if any of this is due to me. Very many times I've said that Viv Richards is vastly superior to me as a batsman. His flick through mid-wicket, for example – I don't think anyone else can do that. Probably it is unique, probably it is a stroke so beyond anyone else that Viv has not changed anything because he is *too* good. No one else can bang good length balls on off-stump through the leg side without ever missing. It's downright unfair. After all these years I've still not worked out how he does it. He says his own way of playing developed in the games he played as a kid, influenced by their rules, and he's stuck with it. He used to play with thirty other kids on bumpy pitches. They'd huddle around the batsman and you could be out one hand, one bounce. So you learnt to play with a dead bat or to hit the ball over everyone's heads, which is how Viv still plays. His way is incomparable and inimitable. Mine is simpler, less dependent on eye, more dependent on violence. You may say he is a murderer with the bat. Well, if that is so, I'm a hooligan!

CHAPTER FIVE

Bumpers

Did you see the Australian television series on bodyline in 1985? Had you ever seen anything like it? It was utterly compelling and yet totally ludicrous. Was it really how people imagine Test cricket to be? It was, of course, a soap opera. Faces smiled to the camera, and ribs cracked like Twiglets as cricket balls hit them. Bodyline's *dramatis personae* included an Indian straight out of Kipling; a public school prig from *Brideshead Revisited*, several Orwellian miners and a group of Australians who, we must suppose, had been lifted from the scenes at Gallipoli (where the English apparently drank tea as slouch-hatted Australians died). Despite these absurdities, the series was peculiarly gripping, and for seven-and-a-half hours it was watched by millions of people.

There is no need to go back fifty years to find bruises, bumpers and danger. Bodyline bowling has been dominating international cricket since 1974. Batsmen feel as soldiers must have when the machine-gun replaced the rifle. The odds have changed. Really the only difference between the 1932–33 attack of Australia and that of the modern West Indians is the field placing. The Clive Lloyd and Vivian Richards artillery bangs the ball in short. No fieldsman is placed to defend the drive. There are slips, gullies and short legs and the bowlers concentrate upon forcing the batsman to defend his body. In isolation, most balls which take wickets are not dangerous. As we watch the news at night we can sit in our chairs and ask 'how in the hell did he get out to that one'? It is the barrage which takes wickets: there is no easing up as the bowlers tire. Cricket has changed. This is the new bodyline. It has been practised since 1974 yet it has largely been ignored.

In the summer of 1985, Rose's arm was broken while Felton, Wyatt and myself suffered broken fingers. I speak only of Somerset. In the winter Jerry Coney denounced the West Indian bombardment during which his arm was broken. Batsmen wear helmets, with those grilles which make you feel like a parrot; they wear arm-bands, thigh guards, and gloves. Meanwhile heads are shaken, as if Tarzan had put on a vest. These precautions are regarded as a sign of lack of courage. They are nothing of the sort. Very few cricketers are frightened of fast bowling; a few suffer from a nervous reaction more akin to shellshock than fear, but cowards are rare. They would not survive a month. It is the game which is different. The odds *have* changed. It takes only one error to break a bone or, worse, to fracture a skull. Cricket is not so much a battle of wits in 1986, as a brutal assault, or at least so it is against the West Indians. Other nations, led by Hadlee of New Zealand and Ellison of England, are returning to the principles of line, length and movement. Even Australia, with Lillee and Thomson in retirement, has turned to fast-medium men in Reid and Davis. Their team cannot sustain the barrage – yet. One day they too will bowl only fast bowlers and then what sort of a game will cricket be? For the time being anyone who has played against Lloyd's or Richards's bowlers has had his courage tested in a way hardly matched in cricket since Larwood, Bowes and Voce.

Botham's courage is not in doubt. He's crashed cars, threatened to jump out of aeroplanes (surprisingly, he intended to wear a parachute), thumped oafs and hooked bumpers off his eyebrows. He is far too much of a crackpot to be a coward. In 1984 he decided to attack the West Indies bowling. He wanted to disrupt the field, wanted to see Lloyd scratching his head. So often the West Indians take the field and march to their places as if by habit. They play to a formula: bowl short, prevent drives, aim at off-stump and place your men in the slips. In India late in 1983 Sunil Gavaskar had tried to upset this cosy tactic by attacking wherever possible. He had failed several times, falling to Marshall's searing pace, a pace excited by the desire to avenge the World Cup defeat earlier that year, but Gavaskar had struck a century, a brilliant 90 on a bad pitch and then 236 not out (the innings during which he reached his thirtieth Test century). This innings, described by friends from Bombay Gymkhana, began with three disdainful fours off Marshall's first three balls. At once Marshall marched around the wicket, firing bumper upon bumper at the batsmen. Gavaskar took these blows upon the chest, staring at Marshall, unflinching. He continued his assault until Marshall retired to long leg whereupon Gavaskar resumed his more usual rhythms, waiting until Marshall returned, ready to strike him once more. By all accounts it was a great and an intrepid innings. It must have been – Gavaskar's mother has it on videotape!

Gavaskar was in England in 1984 and he described his aggressive approach to Botham, who decided that the Indian's mixture of courage and attack could work. The crowd had chanted 'never awaken the sleeping tiger' as Gavaskar went for his shots. Maybe it'd work for Botham too. In the 1984 series, it nearly did. Unfortunately the pitches were poor, and though Botham averaged 36 (second only to Lamb) he did not score his first hundred against the West Indies. He threw away his wicket several times with a century in his reach. But his was the prized wicket still. Gone was the old shuffling across the stumps, the odd, indecisive movements with which he'd played fast bowling in the past. He stood still and hit hard.

In 1985 Botham played Marshall and his friends with disdain. It appeared certain that he would succeed magnificently in the Caribbean that winter.

In November he began his amazing charity walk. He enjoyed himself immensely. He was in good male company. He was a part of a warm team. He could enjoy himself hugely every evening. Around him gathered lots of young and working people with whom he could relax. Striding at a steady four miles per hour from John o' Groats to Land's End, urging on his mates, heralded by stars from other fields, befriended by children who were suffering from leukaemia, drinking tequila with the thirst of an animal in the desert, Ian finished his walk by jumping into the sea off Land's End in top hat and tails. It took him 35 days to complete the 874-mile journey. He raised £710,000 for a charity for which his emotional commitment is genuine. He even missed the birth of his baby, and he returned home having shed nearly a stone! Really, this heroic walk offered to Ian everything he required in life. He didn't even have to play cricket!

Beyond doubt, Botham was not looking forward to the Caribbean tour with nearly as much enthusiasm. He'd have to play cricket, he'd be seen in a more unkind light, and inevitably he would face a blasting from the fast bowlers.

His worst fears were confirmed. After a summer of promise against the Australians England were slaughtered in the West Indies. On a tricky pitch in Jamaica, Gower's men lost by 10 wickets, with Patterson, a raw recruit who'd played for Lancashire and Tasmania, taking 7 wickets in the match. Botham scored 15 and 29, twice falling to Marshall. He took 2 wickets, those of Garner and Richardson, in the West Indies' only innings of substance. Gatting did not play. His nose had been broken when he mis-hooked Marshall. His nose was spread across his face and, apparently, bits of bone were found in the ball. Edmonds played but, regrettably, he was hurt by an accidental beamer from Patterson and ended the match with his chest badly bruised. He scored 5 not out and 7. There's quite a lot to be said for walking, even in November.

Botham did not do well in Trinidad either, though the pitch

was much safer. As usual his failures were more dramatic than anyone else's (no partnership has survived a full session against the West Indies attack for five years). His bowling was punished: his 9·4 overs cost England 68 runs. To Botham punishment is a red rag. He lost his wicket hooking in the first innings, and of course this was roundly condemned. In the second he fought valiantly but was beaten by a superb leg-cutter from Marshall. As he left the field he gesticulated angrily at the press box as if to say 'Well, I tried it your way. See what happens?' It did not help that he'd heard during this Test match that police in Devon and elsewhere were pursuing enquiries into his private life as he walked through Scotland and England. He'd thought that this deed, at least, might be regarded as honourable if not sacred. Something which had been so inspiring had now been dirtied. His cricket did not appear quite so serious after this.

In Barbados, a game approached by the Englishmen with the enthusiasm an old trooper has for a charge, he bowled well, but failed with the bat. England scored 189 and 199 but did not suffer any serious injuries. On the third night Botham went in to bat with twenty minutes left to play. He swished, to the anger of the critics, and was out in the last over. Again he was attacked. At least these comments were legitimate, concentrating upon his cricket. Yet he'd been out pushing at Garner, edging a catch to Dujon. If he'd been reckless he might not have lost his wicket.

England lost the series easily, and in none of these three vital Test matches did Ian prove his ability against fast bowling. He'd succeeded neither in 1984 nor in 1986, nor really when he was captain. In fact his record against the West Indies when he was captain is not substantially different from his record at other times which does, at least, support his belief that leadership did not affect his game.

What is this block against the West Indies? Why is his record so ordinary against them? Gooch, a rumbustious batsman, and

'Nothing feels different before you go in. It just happens. It sort of clicks.'
Graham Morris

Captains, Friends and Advisers

LEFT Despite the opportunities presented to him at club and country level, he has never convinced his peers that he is a good leader. *Adrian Murrell/All-Sport*

CENTRE Words of advice for the former captain, now performing miracles back in the ranks: the Old Man and the Beefy Lad, Edgbaston 1981. *Adrian Murrell/All-Sport*

BELOW Two long-standing team-mates, Gooch and Gatting, appointed vice captain and captain respectively during the Test series against India in 1986 – but for how long? *Adrian Murrell/All-Sport*

RIGHT 'Losing Ken Barrington was the worst shock of my life . . . He was like the rock of Gibraltar, a really patriotic and totally unbending cricketer . . . Along with Vivian Richards, he's the only person I've ever really listened to.' *Adrian Murrell/All-Sport*

FAR RIGHT J. K. Lever, his first England room-mate and a close friend. *Graham Morris*

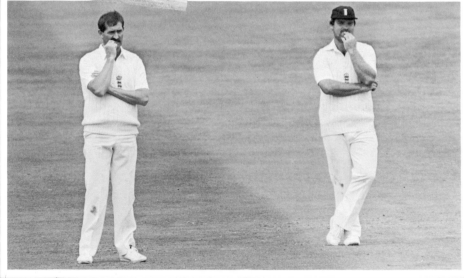

If it hadn't been for cricket ... *Bob Thomas*

Three Somerset Batsmen

TOP LEFT 'Martin Crowe is a perfectionist. He wants to do everything right; every stroke must be just so . . . but he won't be great until he stops being a perfectionist and starts mutilating the bowlers.' *Graham Morris*

TOP RIGHT Sunil Gavaskar, showing that a mixture of courage and attack could work against the West Indies in India, 1983. Botham deliberately followed his example in 1984 and 1986 but failed to achieve the same success. *Adrian Murrell/All-Sport*

LEFT 'Viv Richards is the greatest player because he dominates mentally and physically. He doesn't care about anything else.' *Graham Morris*

Two Yorkshiremen

RIGHT Geoffrey Boycott: 'His average is like a sword. He fights off the world by brandishing it.' *Adrian Murrell/All-Sport*

BELOW Brian Close: 'An extraordinary man, lots of guts, tough as old boots and then, on the spur of the moment, rash.' The two have a lot in common. *Patrick Eagar*

The All-Rounder

TOP LEFT 'Neither in cricket nor in life do I ever want to half-hit shots.' *Sport and General*

TOP RIGHT The Golden Arm. 'The secret of bowling lies in the wrist. I try to break the wrist as late as possible, hopefully after my arm has passed my ear. The later your wrist snaps, the more life you give to the ball.' *Bob Thomas*

BELOW Gomes c Botham b Ellison, The Oval 1984. One of his favourite catches: 'You've no idea where the catch is coming from, it could be low, could be wide, could be straight (like this one). Might as well relax until you see it.' *Adrian Murrell/All-Sport*

The Rest

TOP LEFT One of the greatest fast-bowling feats of all time: Malcolm Marshall bowling England out in the second innings at Headingley in 1984 with a plaster cast on his left arm. *Adrian Murrell/All-Sport*

TOP RIGHT Clive Rice, winner of the Silk Cut all-rounders trophy two years running, proving that it pays to study the rules of the competition. *David Munden*

BELOW LEFT Kapil Dev has recently mastered the art of captaincy to add to his already potent armoury of medium-fast swing bowling and attacking batting. *David Munden*

BELOW CENTRE Imran Khan, despite nagging injuries, an awesome athlete, a glorious fast bowler and a useful Test batsman. *Adrian Murrell/All-Sport*

BELOW RIGHT Like a representative of the Inland Revenue, Richard Hadlee exacts everything on offer. *Adrian Murrell/All-Sport*

LEFT Botham and Hudson: Tim was refreshing but soon the drink lost its flavour. *Graham Morris*

BELOW Fame is a heavy burden to carry, even for a scorer. What price a quiet life outside the game? *Adrian Murrell/All-Sport*

Ellison, a swing bowler, have succeeded. Lamb, Ian's great friend, has done well. So why not Botham? Maybe he really does play too wildly too often. Maybe he does risk too many cross-batted shots. Perhaps he is not quite as good as Gooch or Willey or Lamb at moving into position behind the ball. It cannot be a matter of courage, it cannot be that Ian is thrown by having his friend, Richards, fielding in the slips. Probably his technique is at fault. His choice of strokes may be too bold. The better the bowling, the less faults the batsman can afford. And Richards's bowling is lethal. Against the West Indies Ian seems either to get caught hooking or to edge towards the slips. If he could move behind the ball and hit straight he might score more runs. But there again, he might not. It's an easy game sitting here theorizing about Botham. But it's a dangerous trade: as soon as anyone does that he confounds them. I think I'll let him speak for himself.

Ian's Story

Really what you need to discover is how to play fast, short-pitched bowling. The West Indians grow up with it. In Australia the pitches are hard and bouncy, so the batsmen learn vigorous techniques which include hooking and ducking. Here – who faces a bouncer until he plays in first-class cricket? You don't see them in school or in club games. Apart from anything else the pitches are slow and help seamers, so that fast bowling is killed off, and batsmen survive by using the forward push. You have to learn the game from scratch when you enter first-class cricket.

The game has certainly changed. People who say they'd stand there and sway out of the way are living in cloud-cuckoo-land! Lots of spectators are heroes, and there are a few in the press box too. They would soon be sorted out if they were to hear the whistle of the ball past their noses. I heard Leslie Ames say he received only a handful of bouncers a season. We get that many in half an hour. We wear helmets for the same reason that racing drivers do, to save our lives. Those Australians in 1932–33 are the only fellows who understood the problems of batting against the West Indians in Tests and county cricket. The only difference now is that only two fieldsmen are allowed behind square leg so they bowl straight with two fellows in the deep to stop the hook and a man at short leg to catch the inside edge. Everyone else is in the slips, and the tactics are to bang the ball into the pitch as fast as possible, drive the batsman back, and entice an edge. It works magnificently. Sometimes too many short balls are bowled – for example when Close took Holding on the chest in 1976. Every ball was pitched halfway down. Close arrived at our next game with his body covered in cruel bruises. Willis hit him and his legs buckled. He was still our top scorer. I've never admired a man so much. He wouldn't wear a helmet and he was an incredibly, almost dementedly, brave man.

Few men are prepared to get killed on the cricket field, yet that is the risk you take every time you step out to bat against these fellows. Every ball could remove your teeth. Cricket is a physical game, a game of danger, but that doesn't mean you cannot take precautions. Usually I wear a helmet when I face the West Indians. This cushions blows on the temple and top of the head, areas where lasting damage can be done. One can still be hurt badly – my chin, teeth, nose are unprotected. It amazes me when commentators say that the helmet has slowed batsmen's reactions. You are still in tremendous danger. It isn't only your head – your arm can be broken, or your ribs. Racing drivers don't think, 'Oh, well, I'll take this bend at 240 mph and, if things go wrong, this helmet will save me'.

So many old players do not understand this. They see the game through a fog of their own experience. They remember facing Lindwall and Miller, or Hall and Griffith, remember doing well and then suppose they could bat just as well now. But it is not so easy. They don't realize they'd be playing Lindwall and Miller every day of the season and every hour

60

in the series. At the start of our series against the West Indies in 1984 the press asked if I was going to wear a helmet. I said 'Yes'. They said 'Why?' I said 'Because I'm twenty-eight and I've got a family and I want to see tomorrow'.

At Weston in 1981 we had to face Cowans and Hughes on a dangerous pitch. Viv's first ball from Cowans spun his cap around. I was out first ball. I had backed away a yard to square leg, swiped and missed. Viv said he'd had enough of this bravery/ignorance thing and I agreed. You begin in the game determined to prove yourself a man, determined never to take a backward step. You are like a boxer in his early fights, he's always going to knock the other fellow out. Later he learns some ringcraft, he learns to look after himself, to pick his moment. We are boxers who fight every day. Every day someone is trying to cuff us on the head. You realize that your heroism is rubbish, pure vanity. You realize that if you're going to survive in a battle you don't throw away your shield and lead the charge.

The pitches don't help either. Bad wickets force you to wear a helmet even more than fast bowlers. You can't rely on the bounce – the ball might rise too steeply, or it might squat down. In a game with little margin for error it is cruel that you are playing on uneven surfaces in Headingley, Trent Bridge, Edgbaston and Old Trafford. At Headingley in 1984 you could not tell whether a ball would grub or jump. Marshall took 7 wickets, 3 of them lbw with grubbers. We turned on the telly and people – men who had played the game – were asking why we did not push forward.

When we returned from the West Indies tour, after nine Test matches in a row against Marshall, Holding, Roberts and Garner, we turned up at Old Trafford and there was Michael Holding sauntering in on another dreadful pitch. I said to my partner, Roebuck, 'I'll never survive this over'. I didn't. I was out first ball. As I walked back the crowd laughed. I thought, well that's terrific. I shouted to them 'It's just like the bloody winter' and they laughed again, this time in sympathy. They weren't so bad.

People have said I don't play fast bowling well. You cannot play it at all unless you are in magnificent form. Against the West Indies you must be totally confident. Runs do not come easily, no full tosses, hardly any half-volleys. Any weakness is exposed, especially as they work you out during the series. In the first Test they probe away, at the new players especially, spot a fault and then hammer away at it until either you correct it or are broken by it. I used to be lbw to Joel Garner, getting too far across. Ken Barrington took me to the nets with a bowling machine. He'd tell me to bat on leg-stump to avoid lbws and to move into position without going too far across. He said the best players of quick bowling stand still as the ball is delivered. So I'd move early and wait, giving myself an extra moment to judge the ball and avoid shuffling about. I enjoy batting against the West Indies now. In 1984 I kept getting out to Baptiste. It's marvellous, isn't it? You work out how to play Marshall and Garner and then get out to the medium-pacer!

The West Indians are amazing. They went to Australia in 1975 thinking that cricket was a nice game and that bouncers were supposed to be hooked. A few months later they understood that cricket is hard and they've hardly bowled an over of spin since. Lillee and Thomson changed cricket; certainly they changed West Indian cricket. They bat in the old way, going for their shots, hooking anything short but their attitude is different. They might smile as if they're in a calypso band but inside they are hard. Some of them didn't want to play on that tour. David Murray was reserve wicket-keeper and he said he wasn't going to be challenging Deryck for his place!

Lillee and Thomson were too fast to hook, especially with the new ball. Suddenly the game wasn't fun, the West Indians were at the wrong end of the coconut shy. Michael Holding burst into tears once, and at a press conference Clive Lloyd severely criticized the umpires. They left those shores as angry and beaten men. Lloyd felt they had been a soft touch. Right, he said, I'll put an end to that. He found his fast bowlers, set his field and the rest has followed. Now it is the Australians who are on the receiving end. They are terrified of batting first. The authorities are reluctant to let the West Indians play at Perth. The boot is firmly on the other foot and it has been for ten years.

In 1984 we lost 5–0 to the West Indies. I cannot understand why we played on such dangerous pitches. To have the slightest chance against that lot you must play on slow seamers which help our bowlers. You have to be able to bowl out Richards and the rest for around 300 because you cannot expect to score more than that yourself. On slow, green pitches you have a chance – Marshall and Holding might not be more effective than Allott and Botham, or even Gooch. Yet we played them on wickets of uneven bounce. The fellows who prepare, or order, this type of pitch should strap on the pads and bat on them.

Realistically, we don't have much chance of beating the West Indies in a long series. To score a hundred can take seven hours or 90 overs of fast, short-pitched bowling. You cannot do that more than twice in a series because you simply do not have the nervous energy. That is why Clive Lloyd and Viv Richards believe they cannot lose a five-match series. Our best chance is to choose aggressive batsmen. It is no use picking fellows like Chris Tavaré – a good player and a great lad – because he scores off half-volleys as he is not going to get any. He could bat well for an hour and score 9. Boycott used to do that in 1981. He'd play with immense skill and courage, I mean he'd play really well in his way, and then he'd be out to a snorter. Caught Lloyd bowled Croft 13. There's no future in that. Gooch and Willey are England's best players against the West Indies. Gooch's technique is interesting. He sets himself to go after the ball so that if it is anywhere near a full length he will strike it. His theory is that there are no men in defensive positions and, even if he does edge the ball, it'll take some catching.

Batsmen tend to be of two types: those who are prepared to deal with late movement (Boycott is the master here, he waits for ever before committing himself) and those who want to hit the ball hard. This second type is vulnerable on damp pitches which encourage movement off the seam – pitches typical to the north of England. If you are committed to driving a ball as it rises, and it moves or keeps low, you are in trouble. If, on the other hand, you wait, you can adjust. Brian Close used to say he didn't play the first line of the ball, he'd wait till it had finished moving and then choose his stroke.

In the West Indies it is usually possible to hit through the line of the ball. They used to roll the pitches out there till they shone, and then roll grease or something into them so that you could see your reflection. This has changed. Now, groundsmen prepare pitches to suit bowlers. In the past the West Indies did this less than anyone else. Trinidad helped spinners, and Antigua was a good batting wicket. Only in Barbados, where the groundsman is one of Joel's mates, were things any different. There you'd practise on excellent pitches and then begin a Test match on long green grass with the ball whizzing past your ears. We would do the same if we had the bowlers.

This winter (in 1986) we had a lively pitch in Jamaica, with the ball bouncing all over the place. That's the worst thing in cricket. You can play movement, but if the bounce is uneven then you have little chance of survival: especially if the bowlers hurl it down at 90 mph all day! Trinidad wasn't so bad, though we didn't bat well. I wasn't ashamed of my efforts there. The press were calling for my head in England; the *Daily Mail* had arranged an investigation into my walk. But these events didn't affect my performances. In the second innings Marshall got me out with a fast leg-cutter. They might be able to play those in the press box but I'm afraid I can't.

Patterson was a shock. We'd bargained for Holding, Marshall and Garner. We'd heard about Gray and a couple of others. Next thing you know, Holding's injured and they call up Patterson. We'd played against him in Manchester and he'd been quick but raw. At home he was lethal. He was hungry, young and urgent. Marshall, Holding and Garner are thinking bowlers. Certainly they are fast, but they are masters too; Holding and Garner in particular are supreme technicians. They prefer to take their wickets with skill. Joel doesn't really want to bowl fast, it's not in his nature. Once against Kent in a quarter-final we told him that Alan Ealham had said he had got steep bounce, but couldn't be described as fast: he was that day! He just needs a little stirring up. Holding is the same. In 1984 he bowled off a short run. He fancied he was getting on a bit and decided to pace himself as Lillee and Hadlee had done. Also he was following his horses. Then he met a friend on the way to The Oval, and this bloke said he'd been to every Test match and all he'd ever wanted to see was Holding's full run. Michael nodded and said he might give it a go if he remembered. In mid-afternoon the thought suddenly struck him, he put back his mark and sauntered in, silently, head rolling. He bowled us out, of course.

But Patterson is not like that. He is rough, fierce and fast, like a boilermaker or a coal miner. He was explosive on that heavy pitch in Bridgetown. Even Marshall is sophisticated in a way; he's a real worker, he never gives up, and he's extremely fit and very fast – but he's still like a well-designed car, sleek and shining. You can play fellows like him, you aren't quite as frightened because they are predictable. Patterson was so raw, so full of hatred, like Croft and Clarke used to be. I expect he's a lovely bloke off the field.

I suppose Marshall is the best of the West Indies bowlers, through a mixture of ambition, intelligence and pace. In 1984 he broke his arm. At Headingley, it was. We were doing all right as a matter of fact. They were all out by lunch one day.

Our lads strapped on their pads, relieved not to have to face Marshall on this bloody awful pitch. Then there he is, arm in plaster, dropping his sling and warming up in front of the pavilion. He took 7 wickets. Now there's a fast bowler for you. He wants to be recognized as the greatest bowler in the history of the game. He bowled England out with an arm broken: I'd say that isn't a bad start.

When I retire I'll miss the great camaraderie I've had with the West Indians. I've enjoyed their company. They laugh a lot and play in a happy atmosphere. I won't miss facing their bowlers, though; I think maybe that's a task for a younger man! I've never scored a hundred against the West Indies. One day maybe I will. I had several chances in 1984, and threw them away. What I need is one of those days at the crease when you just know you aren't going to get out. This happened to me against India at The Oval in 1982. I was out for 208, and of all my dismissals this is the one I most regret. It's much worse being out for 150 or 200 than it is for 20 or 30. With those scores you should go on for ever. I could have scored 400. No, I *should* have scored 400. I told Gavaskar I was going to score 200 – I bet him £10 – I should have said 400! He said I'd never have the patience, but that would have kept the little beggar quiet, wouldn't it?

CHAPTER SIX

The Golden Arm

At sixteen none of us thought he could bowl. Dennis Breakwell and Vivian Richards – his flatmates in 1974 – observe that they did not expect him to be more than a useful county batsman. And yet he has taken more than 350 Test wickets, including 5 in an innings twenty-six times. In Botham's turbulent career this is the most difficult thing to explain. Why was it that so many good judges overlooked his talent?

Perhaps it was his exuberance, his optimism. We studied his technique in 1974, and remarked upon his wayward run up and obvious inswinger (he might as well have waved to the batsman to warn him). We did not see the zest which unsettled the batsman as he awaited the youngster's next insult to orthodoxy. There was no pattern to Botham, no 5 outswingers then an inswinger, none of that. It was the same with Chandrasekhar, the Indian spinner. Asked how he decided whether to bowl a leg spinner or a googly he said: 'As I'm walking back I think maybe I'll bowl a googly. Then, as I run in, I think, no, I'll bowl a leg spinner. Then, d'you know, just as I prepare to bowl I decide it'll be a googly after all. And then as I let go of the ball I say sod it, I'll bowl a top spinner.'

Botham was a maverick bowler, his imagination unrestrained by respect for proper conduct. He did not want to impress anyone, he just wanted to take wickets. Nor did he mind much how expensive they were. Sometimes he bowled as an oil-rich Arab shops. That is why he could not copy

Cartwright. Botham persevered with his demented swingers because they were a lot more fun. He could swing the ball, he could bowl all day and he did not mind being driven. He was prepared to attack, to risk punishment for a tumble of wickets.

Botham criticizes Hendrick for being too cautious. He cannot understand Hendrick's reluctance to pitch the ball up. I suggested that he might not want to be driven, to which Botham scornfully replied that if the ball was moving that is what a bowler must want. In truth, it is what an extrovert bowler, a bowler who will not worry if his plan fails, wants.

Ian's other asset as a bowler in 1974 was that he was not taken seriously. Surely this raw, random fellow could not bowl? Professionals admire skill and shudder at bowlers who are inaccurate: these are amateurs who will turn in a few good efforts and many poor ones. And so, whenever Botham was brought on to bowl, they thought they could slaughter him. They almost wanted to show the upstart that you could not trundle down such rubbish and expect to be paid for it. That was how Botham bowled Barry Richards in a Benson and Hedges match. Richards was stunned, turning to accuse Derek Taylor of knocking off the bails, scarcely believing that he could have fallen to such a ball. In his first Test match Botham, after an embarrassing first spell, dismissed the mighty Greg Chappell with a long hop which Chappell, to his dismay, touched onto his stumps. After that Botham bowled well, swinging the ball late to defeat Marsh and taking 5 wickets in his first Test innings. No one else would have bowled so dreadful a first spell. Few others would have seized upon that first bit of luck with such joy.

Botham's bowling ability was underestimated for years. But he is not so effective a bowler now; he finds it hard to take wickets even in county cricket. For his effect he depended upon a potent mixture of lively movement and long spells. He is older now and more prudent (these things are relative) and batsmen are used to his ways. It is not surprising that some performers begin to parody themselves, reproducing a remembered image of a lost originality. Botham at times resembles an ageing comedian condemned to repeat the jokes with which he won his fame, delivering the punchline which everyone already knows. There is a limited number of variations in cricket. Perhaps, too, a little of that spirit, which used to sweep aside batsmen like a strong gust of wind uproots trees, has been lost. Ian does not enjoy cricket quite so much, does not enjoy charging in over after over. It is gruelling work and he's been at it for ten years. He is not quite as good a bowler technically, either. In 1974 he was a slight lad, his body was wiry rather than mountainous. He was not a genuine fast bowler; his wickets were won with movement, with changes of angle and pace. Swing bowlers are rarely heavy men for they rely upon trunk rotation rather than brute force. As they fill out they lose a little of their whiplash.

Ian remains a formidable bowler though, still proud and dangerous in Test matches. He remains unwilling to defend and so is often punished, conceding 4 or 5 runs an over. But Willis, Gower, Brearley and Fletcher invariably tossed him the ball when they were in trouble. Their hope, so often justified, was that Botham could work some miracle beyond the nerve and imagination of others. He has, after all, often rescued England with a devastating burst, which isn't bad for someone who can't bowl.

Ian's Story

Cricket gets harder as you go along. Probably it's the same for other sportsmen: wingers in football perhaps find that the full-backs begin to anticipate their every move. People get used to your ways, and the power to surprise is lost. Everyone has a chink somewhere, even Becker and Maradona are not perfect. It is easier for golfers who only have to consider their own form, they do not have the added worry of an opponent working out ways of beating them.

Besides this you tire of your game a little. You grow up dreaming of playing at Lord's or Wimbledon, dreaming of being a champion. Then, suddenly, you are a champion. People are analyzing you, writing articles about you, dreaming up ways of defeating you. You arrive full of confidence, totally convinced nothing can hurt you, then suddenly people are finding dents, suddenly you realize you are expected not merely to reach that level but to keep up to it. That is when the problems begin. You arrive at the top due to drive and ambition: it's very hard to retain that drive and that ambition when you've made it. Bjorn Borg, for example, retired at twenty-six. He'd won Wimbledon, been world champion. What was left, except to be shot down by the next fellow who came along? He'd worked incredibly hard to get to the top, worked for years, hours every day. He'd taken from tennis everything it had to offer, and given a lot too. New men were appearing as dedicated as he once was, ready to work fanatically to beat him. He didn't have so much to give any more so he packed it in: quite right, too. I don't think you improve with experience. You might learn a few tricks, a few short-cuts, but these only disguise your mistakes.

This is what has happened with my bowling. I don't think it has changed much, not substantially. After twenty Test matches I had 100 wickets and 1,000 runs. It's impossible to keep up that level, day after day, and under so much pressure. Batsmen get used to you and, worse still, you get used to yourself. When I was younger I used to run in wondering what the hell I'd do. I didn't have a plan or anything, things would suddenly happen. Now, at times, I run in and try to remember what I used to do. You begin to impersonate yourself. How was it I bowled out Pakistan that time? You hang on to the past and hope that it will repeat itself.

I've changed physically, too. My shoulders have broadened with all the work I've done but my waist is the same as when I married. There was a time in Australia when I was overweight – the papers printed some photos of me looking like Cyril Smith. When I saw them I realized I was carrying too many potatoes. The funny thing was I felt strong on that tour, really strong. Maybe I was like one of those horses which needs a race or two before it is fully fit.

This physical change has taken place by accident. I was strong as a lad and it was simply a matter of time before I filled out. I've never trained seriously, except for soccer. I don't do weights because I don't like them. I'm big enough as it is and I don't want to get muscle-bound. My strength springs from my life, on the move playing soccer, or golf, or fishing. I do fifty sit-ups a day to correct my bad back which has been painful on and off ever since, like a fool, I bowled a few overs in freezing cold weather in Oxford. I don't believe the injury hinders me, and even if it did I'd never blame it. It's so easy to say, 'Well, you can't expect much from me with this dodgy back'. It's easy to run away – lots of cricketers avoid playing whenever they have a little niggle. I don't believe real men react like that. I've known Viv to play with a broken finger. In the 1985 Benson & Hedges final Paddy Clift played even though he could hardly walk. That is the way champions react. That reminds me of a story about Brian Close. He was hurt in a Sunday League game – he edged the ball into his teeth, losing lots of them, there was blood everywhere, a terrible mess. He arrived on the Monday and sat in the corner, face puffed up, in tremendous pain still. In waltzes Maurice Hill, who knew nothing about Close's injury, and the first thing he says is, 'I've got a hell of a toothache'. Incidentally, Close scored a hundred on that Monday.

I don't think there's any physical reason why my bowling should be less effective these days. If the ball swings less it is because modern cricket balls all swing less. We used to pick up one ball and it would swing a yard, next day we'd have another and it wouldn't go off the straight and narrow. These days each one is tested on a machine. They've changed the centre of gravity too, so that it won't go sideways at all. We used to be able to pick a ball, a nice dark red ball (bright red ones don't swing so much in my opinion), and there would always be a chance of it flying all over the place. Now that they are standardized, the ball usually goes straight whatever colour it is.

On top of this the seams on balls are getting bigger and bigger. Lord's even dictates the number of stitches on each ball as well as the width of them. This encourages bowlers to run in and hit the seam, letting the ball do the work. Why bother to move it in the air when these high seams let you move it off the wicket? Especially on damp English pitches, on which the ball can grip. Australian bowlers cut the ball more by ripping it in their hands – they put life on to the ball because their wickets are hard and do not offer seamers so much help. In Australia the harder surfaces also soften the seams, and once the seam is soft it plops through as if it has hit some rice pudding. Australian bowlers – particularly Hogg, Lawson and Lillee – use their fingers to spin the ball, so that it leaps off the pitch. Here, fellows like Sidebottom and Allott can run in, aim at a length and know that if they hit the seam there is a fair chance of the ball moving one way or the other. None of this applies to the West Indians because they are so extremely fast. But Marshall, Garner, Roberts and Holding are also skilful bowlers who could swing, cut and seam the ball effectively at medium pace if they chose. It isn't a matter of dynamite with them.

I rely very much upon surprise and swing. Well, after years in Test matches, it's hard to be surprising. There are only so many things you can do, like in chess there are only so many openings you can make. I have heard it said that Kasparov is a wild player, but I'll wager his opponents are studying every match he's played so that, sooner or later, they'll be ready for his every move. He won't be able to walk in and amaze them with an idea no one had ever considered before. He'll move his knight and they'll say, 'Oh yes, he did that in Sicily in 1984'.

As far as movement goes, on those days when for no apparent reason the ball does swing I move it as much as anyone. Apart from anything else there aren't many swing bowlers around. Richard Ellison maybe, and J. K. Lever, though he seams it a lot too. Of course seam bowling is more dangerous because, obviously, balls that move off the pitch are moving later than balls which move before they bounce. Also seam bowlers are more economical in that they can bowl to a length. A swing bowler must pitch it up, there's no point in him bowling on a length because that would defeat his movement. You can't beat batsmen with straight balls. Swing bowlers are bound to bowl half-volleys. Good batsmen are not easily beaten by swing, they're more afraid of movement off the pitch, so I must let the fellow drive. If I try to defend it reduces my danger.

I can still bowl fast, as fast as anyone in the England team. At The Oval in 1984 I was quick and I swung the ball. It was humid that day and for some reason the ball swung all over the place. I find I can swing it better both ways. In my early years I relied upon the outswingers, now I bowl at least as many inswingers, especially in one-day cricket when the idea is to cramp the batsman. My inswinger used to be obvious, I'd have to bend over backwards to get it to go the other way. Now that I've filled out, my natural action is more open and lends itself to inswingers more easily. You have to be open-chested to bowl inswingers, which isn't to say that swing is entirely caused by body action. I find that I use my wrist a lot, holding the ball differently using the seam to spin the ball in the air. Sometimes you can spin the ball so that it angles into the bat before resuming its natural course by jumping towards the slips. Also the wrist is vital to pace, every fast bowler uses a late snap of the wrist to produce bounce as well as a couple of yards of speed. Fellows like Garner, Holding and Marshall hold the ball loosely in the fingers. Obviously the more tightly you hold it the less freely it leaves your hand

— and they crack the wrist as they deliver. Really, the secret of bowling lies in the wrist, and even men like Brian Brain and Mike Hendrick relied heavily upon it. I try to break the wrist as late as possible, hopefully after my arm has passed my ear. The later your wrist snaps the more life you give to the ball.

In my early years I did swing the ball a lot, feet at times. I never had a proper run-up though. I'd simply charge in and let go of the ball. My feet used to be all over the place. That changed when I toured with England in Pakistan. Umpires kept calling me for no-balls. I don't believe they were no-balls, I think the rule was being misinterpreted, but we had to accept the decisions. One evening John Lever, Mike Hendrick and I went into the field after a day's play. I marked out my run and for ball after ball I'd run in, examine my footmarks and work out a consistent position. After a couple of hours my feet were landing in the same places every time, and since then I've hardly bowled a no-ball. Oddly I had Greg Ritchie caught at third man in the third Test in 1985 off a no-ball. It was incredibly unlucky considering that I bowl maybe half-a-dozen no-balls in a year, and I was frustrated, so much so that I blew my top. You should never do that on a cricket field, though I was not the first bloke to do so and I will not be the last. We were watching one of those television videos the other day and there was the great Sir Frank Worrell arguing with an umpire. Frank Worrell! The man's practically a saint!

As I said, since that evening in Pakistan I've had a precise run-up. This is bound to make you a more mechanical bowler; when I used to throw down the marker and run from anywhere it helped me to surprise the batsman. Having a set run takes away a little of your inspiration, though it adds to your rhythm and your control, both of which are vital in bowling. You can't go on forever being a bandit, sooner or later you have to start thinking about what you're doing. After I've bowled now you can see the footprints in the grass, as if the abominable snowman had been walking across the field. This isn't a bad thing, though Test batsmen will tell you that they still don't know what I'm going to do next. My bowling now is simply more under control. No one can say I'm a bloke who runs in, bowls a line and length and leaves it at that. With the ball in my hand I'm still dynamic, for better or for worse. I doubt if any bowler in Test cricket has ever taken as many chances as I do.

I never stop believing I will take a wicket. This was one of Lillee's qualities, and Fred Trueman's too, I imagine. If a batsman sees you dropping your head, wanting more defensive fieldsmen, walking back to your mark slowly, he feels he has you beaten. Lillee never gave his foe that satisfaction. He worked out ways of getting wickets. Even if the board said 150 for 1 he still fancied a hat-trick. That is courage in sport – a courage that can never be broken. In the army there's a saying when you're in trouble, 'Wipe your sword and charge again'. I believe in that. I totally believe in that.

If you do badly, if your figures are poor, you feel as if you've let everyone down. Then you realize you tried just as hard as the last time when you took 6 for 40. You have to take the rough with the smooth. A batsman is bound to score runs some time, as long as the bad times don't make him change his ways. If a bowler is good he must fancy his chances and if he doesn't he won't be any good. Good bowlers want to get people out, ordinary bowlers want to return tidy figures, they want it to look right because they are insecure.

When things go wrong it does affect you, though it is important never to let it show. Brearley and I had a real to-do in the second Test at Perth in 1978–79 when I took none for a hundred. We had one more over to the new ball and I was bowling to Toohey. I thought to myself, well, he'll be expecting an accurate over to slow him down before we attack with a harder ball, so I tried a double-bluff. I bowled four bouncers. The first one dropped just where I'd wanted a man. I was furious and he hit the next three to the boundary. Brearley wasn't too pleased. We had a right row, one of our best. I stopped drinking for six weeks after that. Fat lot of good it did me. When things go wrong people always say it's the drink. When you score a hundred they never say, 'Well, that's down to the bottle, isn't it?'

Sometimes I'm punished, sometimes I take wickets, but I never defend. You can't win unless you take a few risks. Like President Reagan said when Challenger blew up, 'The world is for the brave'. I've bowled badly and taken wickets, quite often some people say! On those days, I think of Mike Hendrick, beating the bat all the time. If only he had pitched the ball up. Throughout his career he bowled a foot too short: just a foot. Twelve inches further up and he'd have been a world beater. He might have paid more for his wickets, say 18 apiece instead of 14, but the batsman doesn't have time to adjust. I've seen Hendrick beat the bat four times in an over in a Test match! I said to him, 'Pitch them up and you'll be more dangerous. Take a risk or two.' When we were injured in Pakistan we used to have 'Test matches' in the nets because there was nothing else to do. He'd pitch it up and move it both ways. He'd have six innings to my three, sometimes eight, it depended. He'd pitch the ball up and he was a bugger to play. For some reason he wouldn't do it in matches, though. Maybe it was a matter of nerve. I didn't understand what held him back. He's a magnificent bowler and yet he never took 5 wickets in a Test innings. He never bowled badly, never needed to hide his head in the evening, but he never won Test matches either. He stopped himself being a great bowler.

You never know when bowling will come right suddenly. It won't if you fear failure and change your game. If you compromise, you lose some of the qualities which made you succeed in the first place. If you have doubts then you open up cracks which the world will dive into until they are caverns. To me, a boundary is a gauntlet. It's an insult you cannot ignore. You must sort it out, see who is the better man. I want to get the batsman. Sometimes it goes wrong. That is why I didn't agree with Brearley in Perth. I didn't mind him getting angry, though it's hard to see how he managed it, standing so pleasantly at slip while his workhorse charged in over after over! Toohey took 16 runs off me, but it could have gone the other way. As I said, his first shot went in the air right where I'd asked for a man. It's a risk I've taken a hundred times, punishment for wickets. Sometimes it has worked and sometimes it hasn't.

If you are sensible today, you are sensible every day. Brilliance isn't something you choose, it isn't a switch you can turn on . . . it just happens. It won't if you don't let it, and things going wrong like the Toohey business are done in the same spirit as the things that go right – in the spirit which lifted you to the top in the first place.

In the old days I didn't know what I'd do next. That's all very well to begin with; your first year in county cricket can be your easiest. That is even more the case in Test cricket, because there's more intense study of it. You play a five-match series and everyone's weaknesses are exposed. At every team meeting you examine the same players; and if you aren't good enough yourself you get found out. That is why Test cricket gets harder and harder. I think that is reflected in all players' performances throughout their careers. Who, apart from Bradman, has ended up as convincingly as he began? People forget that.

Also, I am used differently these days. To take wickets in Tests you have to bowl all the time. Over the last two years I have been asked to bowl in short bursts, as a strike bowler. This was particularly obvious in 1985 against Australia. It has never worked for me in any cricket, not even nowadays, not even for Somerset. That's why Kapil Dev succeeds. He bowls in long spells. Obviously it can shorten your career, but I couldn't just be a batsman. I'd get bored in the field.

Attrition bowling is not one of my skills. I have to attack.

It's not as if you ever beat the bat. It's like being a spinner –
you have to force errors. I can remember bowling in Trinidad,
with John Emburey. We were losing and they were scoring
easily. Embers and I bowled for three hours. We bowled something like 60 overs for about 80 runs. We had to bowl outside
the off-stump and it was one of the hardest spells of my career.
It is not in my nature to bowl like that.

I've always wanted to make things happen. Some bowlers
try to start with a few maidens so it looks respectable. Others
bowl the first ball down the leg-side if there's a chance of a
maiden. Hendrick did that in Australia. When we were playing
eight-ball overs he'd fire at least two where the batsmen could
not reach them. They rarely gave wides in Test cricket. It was
a way of protecting his analysis. A lot of economical bowlers
are really defensive. In Test matches you must take wickets
or else you'll be out there all bloody day. Batsmen don't give
themselves up, you have to go and get them. I still try to do
that. Bowling burns up my energy, which is probably healthy
for everyone. Also I don't listen to people who say if I didn't
bowl I'd bat with more responsibility. That's rubbish. I've
always been aggressive and I always will be. Aggressive batsmen are often out to apparently bad shots whereas defensive
players edge one to slip.

If I didn't bowl I'd still want to hit the ball. It has worked
quite well over the years! Anyway I'm not a great batsman,
I've never been a patch on Viv. He is the greatest player and
has been since 1975. I wouldn't be anywhere near him even if
I never bowled another ball. I'd have given my left arm to see
his 322 against Warwickshire in 1985. It's odd, I feel we've
both sharpened our games again. He batted magnificently for
Somerset last year, and I had my best season ever with the
bat. We both fielded well. For some reason we were hungry
again. Maybe it helped Viv to be West Indies captain. A new
challenge can give your game a new energy. My winter off
must have helped me too. Certainly I bowled faster than ever

before and certainly I felt more in control with the bat. I think
if Borg had been able to take six months away from the
treadmill he'd still be playing top-class tennis. It's hard to do
so – there are so many inducements to keep your name in the
papers (not that I was exactly obscure in Scunthorpe) besides
which you never know when you'll break a leg or something
and have your career abruptly ended. There is always that
fear, so you carry on. But my winter's break at home was the
best decision I've made in years. Suddenly I wanted to play
cricket again.

CHAPTER SEVEN

Leading
The Troops

It took Botham nine years to catch his first salmon. Reporters asked him to buy one from a local shop and be photographed with it. They had been told that their newspapers could not afford to send them up to Scotland every year in the hope of Botham finally catching his fish. Botham refused. He was not there to provide a story; besides which, he wasn't going to be beaten by a ruddy fish. Finally, and to his immense delight, Botham landed his salmon. If it had come any earlier it would hardly have been worth the trouble.

In only one area of his life has Ian known failure. He has not convinced his peers that he is a good leader. His England captaincy brought four defeats and no victories. He lost form and his team lost faith in him. Willis, Boycott, Knott and Brearley criticized his rashness; journalists condemned his immaturity. Colleagues regarded Botham as too wayward, and were worried by the intimidating force of his character. They were not prepared to risk their necks by arguing with him.

Botham's appointment as England's captain had been certain. Once Brearley asked not to be considered there was no one else in the team, nor any other senior man in county cricket, to replace him. People had reservations about Ian – he was only twenty-five, was not captain of Somerset and was an instinctive rather than an analytical man. Still, he might be the sort who could say 'follow me, men' and the men would follow. It might work. In any event the selectors dared not deny Botham something he wanted so much. Somerset could not deny Ian in 1984, and had not denied him his cap in 1976. England and Somerset hopes depended upon Botham's humour and spirit. If he were not appointed he might be unable to raise his game, he might sulk.

His experience as England captain shocked and changed Ian. He returned to Somerset a harder, more stubborn man. His resignation was, he believed, forced upon him by powers which had always objected to his vulgarity. He hated collars and ties; and he suspected that the wild kid from Yeovil had been returned to his proper station by those for whom collars and ties were more important than anything else. He took the captaincy naively, but did not leave it so.

As is related in the next chapter, Richards's experience was similar in securing the West Indies captaincy. In Australia, he had sent Gabriel from the field after a lapse and the board regarded Richards as too uncompromising, a man who would follow his own opinions. Lloyd was a diplomat, Richards was not. Both Ian and Viv were regarded with caution by their respective authorities. If they were appointed, what might follow? Certainly they would demand total control, and certainly they would not stand for any nonsense. They were both rigorously honest and outspoken, perhaps not to be trusted with so responsible a position. Neither had hidden his contempt for certain aspects of cricket's governing bodies. Could not some more amenable characters be found?

England appointed Gower, a mild, amiable, slightly sardonic man, who might serve until a more formidable candidate emerged. The West Indies appointed Richards in the end, and he has succeeded, playing his cricket in a hard, utterly uncompromising manner. Botham was less certain of himself, less willing to stand apart and to dictate. Whereas Richards's cricket was rejuvenated by his appointment (he'd been so tense about it for years, believing a conspiracy of 'polite' men would deny him his just deserts), Botham's character was inhibited. He fretted, and he is not a man given to fretting. As Richards argues, Botham might have succeeded, given the time. In some respects, Ian is a slow learner. His captaincy was instinctive, often superb, but his judgement of character and treatment of others was poor. He assumed everyone else was simply ready to march out there and get stuck in. He did not understand the complexities of those around him, and so did not know how to charm or bluster them into playing well.

Botham's mistake, though he would not agree, was that he gave his enemies plenty of reasons to sack him as captain. At the time they were right to dismiss him, that is the pity of it. Probably Ian will not captain England again. A sense of failure will linger, a curious failure in a way because his captaincy began with high promise.

Ian led England to a rare victory over the West Indies in a Prudential match at Lord's, lifting his team with a surging unbeaten 30 which included a clout for 6 off Joel Garner. He left the field, his eyes intoxicated with the joy of the occasion, his arms waving. It was the sort of *Boy's Own* heroism we'd expected, as Captain Beefy slashes his team to magnificent triumph. Vic Marks was impressed by Ian's ability to cope with the various details of captaincy – the press, the interviews, the selectors, the decisions – and the confidence he gave to everyone. Marks returned to Taunton full of praise for Botham's command. It was an auspicious beginning to a troubled reign.

England lost that series in 1980, though the crucial Test match hung on Gower's failure to take an awkward catch offered by Roberts. Had Gower held the catch England would have won a Test match and probably a series and Botham would have been praised. As it was his team was outplayed, though never humiliated, and Botham's form was poor.

His appointment to lead England to the Caribbean was expected. With him went A. C. Smith as manager and his close friend, Barrington, as assistant. Smith, like Jackman, appeared to be the sort of fellow who would raise the hackles in Botham's democratic view of things; he affected a silk scarf on the field and his accent had an edge of polo about it. As it turned out, Smith and Jackman won Botham's friendship by their steadfastness. But it was Barrington upon whom Botham relied more than any other man in his life.

Botham played golf with Barrington, listened to him at practices (this distinguished Barrington from almost everyone else), accompanied him for quiet evenings. He sensed in Barrington a warmth and regard that was not as sharply judging as others. He could see that Barrington was not a man who would abandon him when things went wrong. This sort of loyalty is rare, and Botham tries to surround himself with it. His friends – Richards, Andy Withers and a few others – are his friends because they will not condemn his outrages. They enjoy his spirit and do not sit in judgement. Botham says he loved Barrington – a rare admission for so solitary a man. He loved him as an uncle, an adviser and a companion. Barrington's sudden death early on a tour already bedevilled by injury, political wrangles and rain, was a great shock. Botham recalls that most of the England team were in tears as they took the field to begin the Test match in Barbados.

Botham could not have managed as well as he did without the help of Willey, Smith, Stevenson and Jackman – an incongruous mixture of friends who have in common an honesty and a conviction respected by Botham. Willey was particularly helpful, lifting the team by his example and not standing for any long faces. He helped his captain by demanding that everyone get on with the cricket, a vigorous approach appreciated by Botham.

England did not lose the series by an embarrassing margin. The West Indies dominated every match, but twice England avoided defeat, as Gower, Gooch and Willey defied the fast bowlers with centuries. Botham had another poor winter and his team doubted whether he was responsible enough to captain England. In Trinidad he announced that heads would roll if his team lost. The comment was intended as a light-hearted aside, but it was the sort of remark journalists transfer into bellowing headlines, which Botham ought to have foreseen. England lost the match, in part because Botham played a wild heave after an hour's resistance, allowing himself to be caught at deep mid-off off Richards's gentle spinners. It was a second stupid mistake, foolhardy and unworthy of England's captain. It was not surprising, either, that people were quick to point this out.

At last the miserable tour ended. Back in England Botham heard that he had been appointed to lead only in the first Test at Trent Bridge. The match was lost, largely because England dropped even more catches than Australia. Brearley observes that Botham appeared unwilling to bowl himself and that his run-up had developed a nervous hiccup. He even called Botham 'the sidestep queen'. He also noticed, as Richards had done in the Caribbean, that Botham was tense, appeared to be listening for insults rather than imposing himself on the game. Botham appeared inhibited by his thoughts and thus lost confidence.

After one more Test match he resigned. The Lord's Test was drawn, with Botham falling for a pair. So desperate was he that, going out to face Ray Bright in the second innings, he decided to sweep his first ball wherever it was pitched. Unfortunately the ball was straight and Botham was bowled. It was not a dismissal likely to endear Botham to the members at headquarters, and Botham returned, as an England captain can never have done before, to an eerie silence. Three weeks later he was a hero to the nation.

Botham went to inform Alec Bedser of his resignation as soon as the match was over. He 'beat the bullet' by a few minutes, though he denies that this influenced his decision. He says he could not continue on a match-to-match basis since this temporary position was not fair on the rest of the team, let alone his family. He returned to the dressing-room to inform his colleagues, only to discover that most had already hurried off to their various county games. Those that remained were quiet, for there was nothing that could be said.

Eventually Ian jumped into his car and drove at a furious pace to the *Four Alls*, his regular pub in Taunton. There, to his delight, he found quite a few Somerset players awaiting his return, ready for a sympathetic pint. He talked to Viv late into the night and next morning arrived early at the ground for Somerset's cup semi-final with Kent. He went out to the nets at 9.15 and was greeted with a loud ovation. In his first over Woolmer was caught off a long hop and we wondered if his luck had returned. But he didn't do much after that, not until the next Test match at any rate, though he rather made up for things then.

In September 1983, two and a half years later, Ian succeeded Brian Rose as captain of Somerset. It was a position he desperately wanted, and a position for which he fought, believing that he could bring the club to fresh glory. He suspected that others were basking in a light which was rightly his. Once more people had reservations but duly and correctly, Ian was given his chance. His team did very well in 1984, though this was largely because of the magnificent form of Martin Crowe and Vic Marks. It was Crowe who formed the youngsters into a club which met every Thursday at the *Nag's Head* in Taunton, wore blazers to matches and worked hard in the nets. Crowe is a magnificent coach because he has built his own game as an architect builds a house. To the apprentices he was an example and a help. Without his influence in 1985 they were much less successful.

Ian was appointed for a second term. He had gambled and lost once – bringing Dennis Breakwell back into first-class cricket for a cup quarter-final which was narrowly lost, and for which Somerset did not select a single specialist bowler.

In 1985 he gambled a second time. With Somerset plagued by injuries he summoned a lager-drinking friend of his to play against Glamorgan. Luck did not smile upon this gamble, for the friend (one of the best players in local club cricket) tore a muscle before or during the game – it was not clear which, though he had been lying on the physiotherapist's table before taking to the field – and was a virtual passenger in a match which was lost on its last ball. These were devastating blows to Ian's standing in the team. Yet the gambles could have worked, and had they done so Ian would have been a hero and we would all have said that we had agreed from the start.

However, Somerset finished bottom of the championship in 1985. We have been bottom often before, indeed it was the previous six years that were the aberration, not this apparently solitary disappointment. But it was sad after the great expectations of Somerset gaining its first championship trophy. Once more Botham had been unlucky; Rose, myself, Wyatt and Felton all broke bones. Davis lost form and Garner missed most of the season through injury. Ian could not stop this sorry slide. He batted majestically but took only 13 wickets. Too often he was exhausted, appeared unwilling to lead by example as a captain must. If he was cynical about his game then he could scarcely expect his colleagues to rise above the setbacks.

Yet Botham *does* care. He had a vision of a beautiful world at Somerset, where he and his mates, arriving in eccentric clothes to upset the fuddy-duddies, would laugh and drink the nights away, and then storm around defeating all the conventional types with their managers and their serious faces. He wanted his team to play by his own lights, with an anarchic, daredevil spirit. Above all he wanted Somerset to do well. Like Viv and Vic, perhaps even Joel, Ian is more emotionally committed to the county than he'd care to admit. He is at home in Somerset with its disdain for airs and graces, its contempt for vogue, its suspicion of smooth-talking men in dark suits.

But Ian could not communicate his vision, he wanted it simply to happen. Nor did he show his younger team-mates that he wanted his team to do well. They hadn't witnessed his triumphs of the past. They saw only this legend who didn't want to bowl, couldn't talk to them easily and took reckless gambles. They saw his anarchism not as hilarious but as destructive. Ian was an inappropriate leader for a team slowly losing its stirring, independent characters, slowly replacing them with gifted but less forceful men.

Ian did not succeed at Somerset. He was reluctant to speak to his team, unwilling to stand apart to impose standards. He did not want to be distanced from his mates. Oddly this democratic approach is better suited to international cricket, where the players are competent, experienced and able to appreciate Ian's outrages as a part of his formidable temperament. Following his experiences with Somerset Ian is tactically much wiser. If he'd been appointed captain of England for the summer of 1986 he would probably have been superb. Unfortunately the cards did not break that way. Ian was captain when his judgement had not yet separated the gambler's throw from the reckless move, had not yet understood the danger of tarring each player with the same brush. Maybe those lessons have been learnt. Experience is a bitter teacher.

Ian's Story

Being captain of England didn't inhibit or change me. That was just an excuse people offered for poor form and for taking the captaincy away from me. I play better with responsibility. It is easier to concentrate. Being captain coincided with two series against the West Indies and a run of bad scores for me. We lost a few games – not as many as in 1984 or 1986 – and I didn't do well, so people simply put the two things together.

Then when my luck turned in 1981, ironically immediately after I'd resigned, people said it was obvious that responsibility had ruined my game. It was rubbish. Even Brearley said I was happy again at Headingley and that I was laughing hugely. If I was laughing it was because I was in form again. I could easily have failed there. I played and missed and edged and all the rest of it. But that's the way it goes.

I had been in terrible form, it's true. In the second Test, my last one as captain, I was on a pair. I couldn't imagine how I could hit the ball, I couldn't see myself scoring a run. So, as I walked out, I decided to try a sweep whatever the ball was. Ray Bright was bowling. I swept, missed, and was bowled. I walked back. What could I say? The Long Room was incredibly, awesomely silent. No one said a thing. It was a bitter moment, as if I was being shut out. A year before, even a fortnight later, they were clapping. Here no one could say 'bad luck'. They thought I'd let the side down. Did people imagine I didn't feel that too? Did they suppose I was being bad on purpose? I was desperate. It happens to everyone, but my bad trot was used to dispose of me – because, even in form, I was an embarrassment.

Some people talk about 'Botham' or 'Allott' as if they were discussing the labourers on their farm. I used to get angry as soon as I walked into Lord's. I used to feel unwanted, uncomfortable. That Long Room is like a headmaster's study. The members persuaded themselves I was no good as captain. Of course I made mistakes, lots of them, but I'd have been sacked as soon as things went badly anyway. I was abandoned as if I were a hot potato, and I was bitter with the establishment. I was let down. They had known it would be a hard year. Our team was changing with old players slipping out. We were playing the might of the West Indies. We lost here only one-nil and if we had held our catches we would have won the decisive match. In the Caribbean we lost two-nil, which wasn't bad. That is cricket. Then against Australia at Trent Bridge we lost because we dropped catch after catch.

Captaincy is a thing you learn slowly. You learn from your mistakes, which teach you much more (and are remembered much longer!) than your victories. Most of my bloomers were more a matter of indiscretion than tactics. In the West Indies it was not my manoeuvres but my approach which provoked criticism. Yet, when the other team is so much stronger, whatever moves you make are likely to go wrong. You lose, in the end, because the other team holds the aces. You've got a few jacks here and there, but they've got these great big aces and everyone knows it. You try one thing and you lose. Your observers have the advantage of the hypothetical. They can say, 'Well, he shouldn't have done that, you know, if only he'd . . .' and no one can say they're wrong. In my opinion about the only way we could have beaten the West Indies would have been if they had appointed some white colonial as their captain! As it was, they were like Manchester United in the 1960s, when Busby was in charge. They had the best players, they had a great man in charge and they had teamwork. None of Lloyd's team ever put himself above the others; they were a close-knit destructive force with a belief in what they were doing, as dangerous as commandos inspired by religious fervour.

In every respect that first tour as captain to the West Indies was an extraordinary experience. For a start it rained most of the time, so that we could not practise. Boycott, Bairstow and Stevenson found a slab of concrete surrounded by cows and sheep and they practised there! Still, that's your Yorkshireman for you. Everyone else simply tried to keep fit, though it was tempting to lodge yourself in the bar and grumble about the rain. Those islands – St Vincent for example – are like a dreamland. You go for a walk and you lose yourself, just like I do when I'm fishing. With the weather so appalling it wasn't easy to break free of this trance and to remember the corps of pressmen and the enormous publicity your cricket and your every utterance attracts. It was as if we were cut off in an entirely different world, far removed from all the talk in the papers and the speculation in pubs. On tour you hardly ever meet anyone not in some way involved in the cricket. Certainly you never meet anyone who has not heard of you. In Australia I rented a house for my wife and kids so that, at least when I was in Sydney, I could re-enter the real world.

When I started being a cricketer I didn't expect to turn into a monk – yet that's the sort of remote life you lead. Though tours can be full of strange experiences, yet they are very routine too – up, breakfast, stretch, practise, play, bathe, bar, steak, bed. Same company, day in, day out, and none of the papers or football teams or drink you're used to. For five months you are dragged into a different culture, and it takes only a few hours to get there. You are sixteen men with a scorer, a trainer and a couple of managers and it is you against the rest of the world. It doesn't help if it rains all the time – you feel like an explorer who is snowed in, stuck in his tent and forced to contemplate his feet.

When, finally, the sun appeared in the West Indies, we had to send for Robin Jackman and the authorities in Guyana refused to let him play. All sorts of meetings followed from which the managers tried to shelter me but this was my team and I was involved. The players were my responsibility. In Guyana we sat in a hotel for three days doing nothing, getting frustrated and fed up with the interference. Eventually we left there and were just beginning to get into the swing of things when Ken Barrington died. This was a shattering blow, a terrible blow. In Barbados I led the side out and most were in tears. I've lost two close friends, Ken Barrington and Peter McCombe (Viv's friend, whose coffin I was proud to bear), both of them totally unexpectedly. You keep expecting them to reappear, cheery, larger than life. Barrington – the Colonel – was immensely popular, a truly great man.

Those fellows on that tour survived a lot. We fought back to save games with tremendous guts. And to return to England to hear ourselves described as failures, and for me to be condemned as a baby, was terrible. We'd endured a hell of a lot and we hadn't dropped our heads, not once. What did the papers know about that? What do people who sit and watch ever understand about that sort of thing? We had shown a lot of the Dunkirk spirit yet here they were complaining that we lost the fight.

Losing Barrington was the worst shock of my life. He felt the pressure on the players, and it hurt him. The defeats, the politics, the hammering his players were taking, they were like knife-wounds to him. Every day his players had to rise from their beds to face the awesome challenge of the West Indian attack; they were out on their own, criticized by people from the sanctuary of the press box, and he felt for them. He understood how fearsome the cricket was, he understood the courage of his players. He carried every blow upon his shoulders and it killed him.

Without Ken it was left to A. C. Smith and myself to run the show. A.C. was marvellous. I'd been extremely suspicious of him, with all those silk scarves and his education and the feeling that he was an upper-class twit who'd been put in charge because of his background. Of course he was nothing of the sort and before, during and after the troubles I learned to have a high respect for him. He was marvellous, a rare man, who is considerate and kind, altogether a man of quality. I've been lucky with my managers. Doug Insole was marvellous too, and Mr Subba Row. I don't say that because they are a part of the establishment which I want to please, I say it because I mean it. They were straightforward and likeable people who were on the players' side without pretending to be one of the boys.

After Ken died we had a meeting. Geoff Miller was vice-captain. He had been appointed when Willis went home. This was a mistake because he wasn't in the side; Graham Gooch should have had the job. He was the person I wanted but we were overruled from England. Mind you, Miller did a superb job because it was very hard for him, sitting in a team meeting saying 'I shouldn't play'.

We went down to the beach for a chat. We decided that the tour must go on. That's what Kenny would have wanted and there was no point in going home with our tails between our legs. We had to raise the team's spirit which would be hard because a lot of them had had the stuffing knocked out of them. But all the team responded. We tried like hell. It wasn't as if our team was strong either. We didn't have much bowling – though Dilley was very quick when everything fell into place. Apart from him we had Stevenson, Jackman and myself – well, you cannot beat Marshall, Holding, Roberts and Garner with medium-pace, not in the West Indies.

Peter Willey was magnificent. We were close friends – I could go and talk to Pete as I used to talk to Kenny. We'd go for a walk or have a beer. Suddenly the manager was so preoccupied that I had nowhere to escape to. Everything seemed to fall to pieces. It would start to go well and then – bang.

As it happened, the Barbados Test match was an extraordinary game. The pitch is always grassy there, hardly surprising when you remember it is the home of Marshall, Garner, Clarke, Stephenson, Boyce, Moseley and the Lord knows who else. We won the toss. If we'd lost it the game would have lasted two days. It was still hard and green when we batted. Boycott received five balls from Holding that were like lightning flashes. He jumped and parried and danced as if he were standing on hot embers. How he stayed alive, let alone kept his wicket, I cannot say. The last ball of that over was dead straight. Boycott didn't move into line and it bowled him. The ball never moved at all. The crowd simply erupted. The roof would have blown off if there had been one. People fell off trees. The mighty Boycott bowled for a duck! It was a memorable piece of cricket.

A little later I went in. I hooked Garner and said 'fetch that'. I don't know what came over me. Joel never shows anger, but the next ball almost took my head off! I've never faced as fast a delivery, never. Visiting teams don't win in Barbados. The groundsman is a friend of Joel's.

Apart from that, the tour went well. Our dignity was saved and our pride was shown by three incredible innings in the series. In Antigua Willey saved us with an unbeaten century. Graham Gooch hit 116 out of 224 all out in Barbados and there was David Gower's 154 not out in Jamaica. Graham Dilley bowled fast too. He is the only white man in the last few years whom you could say is as hostile, as ferocious, as the West Indians. He was a great psychological boost. The added determination after Kenny's death helped as well. Graham Stevenson bowled for three hours in Antigua with a torn thigh muscle, heavily strapped, and swung the game back in our favour. He was a great asset. He'd bowl for you all day. He spent a lot of time with Pete Willey and that probably helped him because Pete has always been a fighter, a gutsy player.

The captaincy didn't affect my game: something just wasn't working. For ten months my highest score was 40 and my best bowling, 4 for 100. It was the leanest spell I've ever had. I had played for five years and everything had gone superbly. Maybe I was due for a lapse.

Captaincy is a hell of a job, nevertheless. At that time I hadn't even captained Somerset much. I found it easy on the field. Off the field it was difficult. It was a shock, actually – press conferences, speeches, being right in the public eye. It is like living with a television camera following you. My greatest weakness was man-management. I'm not good at discipline either. I hated speaking to the team. But I've learnt about that now – you must treat each player differently. Some fellows you shake up, others you kid. Fletcher does it well – for example, he just lets Pringle look after himself, doesn't worry him, or put any pressure on him. I was insensitive, I realize that now. I suppose I'm like Close, just wanting to get out there and get stuck into the opposition. People said I was a good captain once the game started and not so good before or after.

I'd love to be England captain again but I don't think I ever will be. It's no problem for me playing under other fellows – Fletcher was an excellent captain, and as for David Gower or Mike Gatting, that's no problem either. Because the fellow has something I want I'm not going to say stuff you, make your own decisions. Once that happens you are finished. It's no use begrudging other people things.

My record at Somerset wasn't so dreadful, either. We won the NatWest Cup under my captaincy in 1983, and 1984 wasn't a bad year either. Then 1985 was very difficult. We had so many injuries, and Joel and Viv had to miss a few games early in the season. A month into the season we were in terrible trouble – lots of injuries and already out of two leagues and one cup. On reflection, we expected too much. We'd lost Moseley, Taylor and Denning, and we hadn't replaced them. In addition, because I'd been away so much, I lost my grip on the club. I missed fourteen championship matches. I didn't really know how the lads were. You can read the papers, follow the scores during the day, but these are only figures. I couldn't really tell if a bloke was being unlucky or whether he had a problem. After a Test match I'd arrive in Taunton hoping for a rest, only to find a team of clapped out bowlers expecting me to do all the donkey-work! Quite frankly, I really wanted only to bat. It's bloody hard work taking wickets, especially without support at the other end.

I doubt if a Test player can captain a county team properly. It may be all right for Gatting, who has a hardened, experienced team who will carry on without him; but David Gower has found it difficult at Leicester. It is such an involved job, all those meetings, responsibility for all those players, supposedly interested in each one of them. I was only in

Somerset for about forty days a year. I couldn't help that, but it didn't help me.

I didn't want to resign. I don't believe in resigning from anything, don't believe in running away from a challenge. Right from the start I've accepted any sort of challenge. At Oxford once I tried to hit a six off the last ball of the match and was caught. We had needed 17 to win. Everyone said I was a bloody idiot but I thought, what the hell? It wasn't good for the average, but so what? A lot of people start off with great verve and enthusiasm, and then it peters out – they play the odds I suppose. I've never done that. I couldn't work out the odds if I tried, and anyway it would take all the fun out of everything.

I'm sorry not to be captain of my county. I don't see it as a failure, it was just the turn of events. I'd like another go before I'm done. You can't give in, can you?

CHAPTER EIGHT

Viv and Ian

Viv Richards and Ian Botham met in 1973 in Bath, where Somerset Under-25s were playing Glamorgan. Their friendship has lasted ever since; it is an improbable and enduring relationship between two formidable talents, a rarity in sport.

They are an odd couple. Richards is a private man who used to sleep with a jumbo bat by his bed to deter thieves, a man who bristled with anger whenever Botham left a door unlocked. Botham is open, generous, disorganized, less suspicious, less careful than his friend. Richards dresses immaculately and times his entrances to impress – he is never hurried, preening himself for an hour every morning. Botham's hair is long, straggly and sometimes unkempt; moreover it changes colour from time to time. (Mr Woodcock has suggested that it is bleached by the Scunthorpe sun.) Botham used to dress carelessly, throwing on whatever lay around his bed as he came to life. Now nurturing his cavalier image, he dresses wildly and apparently randomly, though at vast expense. By a slight but critical change, Botham's magnificent contempt for primping and preening has become a fashion of its own. The dandelion has turned into a sunflower.

But the two men had much in common too. They shared a determination to enjoy themselves, throwing themselves into life with a gusto particularly evident in their early cricketing years. They went to pubs, nightclubs and discos. They drank lots of beer and neglected meals. In the meantime their careers brought them glory and wealth and the attendant pressures. Quickly both developed into great cricketers – the best in years – and they revelled in their success, touching heights denied to others as they endured the pressures.

Their lives developed along parallel lines. Both men married, both have children, both employ helpers (though Peter McCombe, Richards's closest friend, died in Antigua in 1984), both are at times bored by the game and both have strained relationships with the authorities.

They admire different things in each other. From the start Botham sensed in Richards a power, a strength that was destined to bring greatness. Richards gives off a heat as a poppy gives off a perfume. He felt that Richards, too, wanted to reach for the sky. Botham's ambitions were no more precise. He respected Richards's refusal to compromise. He saw that Viv intended to succeed, and that he was going to do it his own way, without listening to the lullabies of caution. He was impressed by the West Indian's nonchalance, the fact that he was majestic, imperial, disdainful on the field. These were all characteristics Botham wanted for himself.

Viv quickly realized that he could trust Botham: he sensed Ian's warmth and enjoyed his company because he could see Ian was a down-to-earth man. Richards is wary of peacocks, those who bother with you only if it fuels their own vanity to do so. Viv has played for two unfashionable teams, Somerset and Antigua; he has represented the West Indies, a team previously bedevilled by inconsistency; he still has the friends of his youth, though some are Rastafarian (and so frowned upon) and others are poor. Botham has played cricket for Somerset, soccer for Scunthorpe. He, too, sees old school friends and haunts the pubs of his youth.

They are both determined not to be spoilt. Neither Botham nor Richards has been appointed to lead his country's team without a measure of reluctance. They both think this is because they do not coo and cry to the satisfaction of the elders. Richards has led the Leeward Islands to its first Shell Shield title; Botham has captained Somerset to a cup victory at Lord's, yet still their selectors were not convinced. Richards says: 'I'm a very down-to-earth person and some people want a captain who gets up every morning, puts on his tie and goes out and drinks in the finest of places, who speaks posh. I'm not into all that . . . they want you to be a diplomat; you've got to choose your words. No way. I'm just blunt when it comes to that.'

Ian will echo these sentiments. He thinks his fault is that he does not say or do the right things, does not present himself in the appropriate manner. Neither man believes that there is any weakness that will prevent them maturing into outstanding captains. They are great cricketers; why should they not be great leaders too?

It is not inevitable that inspired cricketers are wise captains. Often their talents are instinctive, relying upon physical gifts and immense determination rather than clever analysis. Ian and Viv developed as cricketers in a natural way. They did not meet difficulties and defeat them by changes of technique: it was more a matter of Ian's strength and Viv's power. On the field they do not bother with subtleties. Ian in particular prefers to bulldoze his opponents, and rarely considers bringing about their destruction by more subtle means. They are men who set an example of commitment and brilliance to which their teams are supposed to respond. Neither man is adept at urging his team with words. Botham, as Somerset's captain, was rarely persuaded to address his team. He suspected that his words would sound hollow, especially in relation to his deeds. Yet both Richards and Botham can be immensely forceful in private, encouraging their friends and giving support to team-mates.

Botham and Richards now also share the difficulties of decline. Botham is thirty, Richards thirty-four, and within a few years they will retire. Richards will no longer be able to stare down bowlers, certain of his superiority. Botham will not be able to turn matches in twenty minutes. Within a few seasons, their volatile careers will be examined and every bout of failure will be scrutinized for signs of deterioration. Already there is some wear and tear – Botham cannot bowl with as much life, while Richards is denied the early authority he requires. Already there have been periods of failure: Richards scored 81 in nine Test innings in 1983–84 and Botham has not shaken a series since 1981.

As Richards has observed, Botham could retire now and still be recognized as a magnificent cricketer. There is very little more for either of them to do except hang on to their thrones. They have found it difficult in the last three or four years to sustain their mastery. They have been less consistent and have heard themselves condemned in several continents; each time they have risen to answer the critics but each time have had a little further to go. To have left the game with their reputations intact Botham should have retired in 1981, Richards in 1979, just as Bob Dylan might have been well advised to die in 1969 or Elvis in 1963. As it is they carry on, knowing they can never again be quite such a force but doing what they had wanted to do from the start.

Ian's Story

Apart from Ken Barrington, who, as I have said, was my closest adviser until he died, the only person whose opinion I seek is Vivian Richards. I don't think it is easy for anyone less than Viv to help me in any way, because they have not experienced the same things. It is difficult to talk to anyone about cricket unless they have played the game to a similar standard. They simply do not, cannot, understand what is involved. Non-cricketers see the game in an entirely different light from cricketers, especially professionals. However imaginative people are they cannot grasp what it is like. It is easier for rock stars or actors, or oil sheikhs, to recognize the truth of what one says than it is for lesser cricketers.

Even in county cricket there is very little common ground between me and the average player. This cannot be avoided. I'm no longer merely a man who can play cricket better than other people. I am a character projected onto a huge commercial stage. Frankly, I think the most famous cricketers are too big to play county cricket. That sounds totally arrogant, but I think it is true. You see, our lives have taken us into unimagined worlds and yet there we are, day in and day out, playing 112 overs of a county match, from morning till night. It's as if a part of us has stood still, as if it is dragging us back to something we left behind years ago. Famous sportsmen these days are not only sportsmen, they are characters in a national and sometimes international drama. We have survived rep, and are playing the great roles on the great stages, except that in between we've got to play bit parts in melodramas in Cleethorpes. Apart from the royal family and Mrs Thatcher I'm probably the most famous person in England. That isn't of my choosing, nor entirely of my making. It is simply so. Yet still I and others like me trot out every day in front of tiny crowds in old-fashioned grounds. It is as if cricket will not recognize that stardom, the glorification and celebration of character, has not happened. We are not artesans any more, we are the heroes. The game is for us and the spectators. Cricket cannot be treated as if it belongs to some stuffy private club in London.

Viv is in the same boat as I am. He realizes what is possible and what is not. We are very close friends, as close as brothers. We were close right from the start, before either of us had made it. I'll never forget the first game I played with him. It was in 1973, an Under-25 game between Somerset and Glamorgan. I was on the Lord's groundstaff and I'd heard about this black fellow who was smashing everyone around in club cricket. He was really quiet, hardly said a word, but you could sense the inner strength. He was skinny, not imposing at all apart from his conviction. Some people have that aura, and you can't take your eyes off them. They say Humphrey Bogart was like that; that there was no point in making a brilliant speech on the front of the stage if he was lighting a cigarette at the back.

Viv was bowled first ball. I made 96. Then I bowled like an idiot and he took 6 for 25. I caught the last one and he came up to me and said, 'You score the runs for Somerset and I'll take the wickets'. He wasn't down at all, he just laughed. I liked his nonchalance: he had so much style, he was so cool. You could see he was cut out to be great, that it was just a matter of time.

Since then the bond has tightened. We are deeply loyal to each other. Both of us, I think, place loyalty above judgement. We stick by each other even if, inside, we are saying 'what's the lunatic up to now?' We feel at times as if it is us two against the world. I suppose from the start I regarded Viv as the only fellow with as much pride, ambition and confidence as me. He can be ruthless and kind, humble and arrogant at the same time. He is a big man, as was Brian Close, as are all men with great qualities and (so I'm told) great faults. Viv is totally independent, he never drops his head, never admits that he may be beaten. He has the courage to back himself against anyone. I admire this quality. He's a hell of a competitor.

Also our relationship is based on physical respect. Richards is the only bloke around (except maybe Peter Willey) who is as strong as I am. He is not intimidated by me, which is why we've never had a serious row. We respect each other as men, as fighters. His power is awesome. It's important to have someone around who will say 'sit down and shut up' and will go on saying it even if you threaten him. Other people would be wary of pushing me too far, and rightly so. Viv will say 'Well, then, big fellow, you want a fight?' In the end, especially in sport, things do come down to brute force. Viv is as brutal as I am, or he could be, if ever either of us chose to use force.

Viv is deeply proud of his origins. He wears those Rastafarian bands as a sort of defiance of all those who say he must abandon his old friends because they are not respectable enough. Viv will not have any of that, and would sacrifice his own ambition to be loyal to those friends. The Rastafarians are poor because they do not believe in property; they live in little tin shacks, and though they will not touch alcohol they do smoke ganga because, to them, it is the herb of enlightenment. Real Rastafarians wear their hair in dreadlocks. Also they never say 'we' because that word hides individuals, so they say 'I and I'. I don't pretend to know everything about the subject (neither Viv nor I are Rastafarians) but he feels he must support them because they are treated so badly everywhere and because so many of them are interesting and unpretentious people. Viv is a man for the underdog, and I respect that, so I wear these sweatbands too, by way of solidarity. They are the colours of the oppressed black man, which is why we have chosen them as the colours we use for our range of clothes too. It is all tied in.

We have helped each other a lot since 1973. I used to go to Bath to see him, and when we joined Somerset in 1974 we shared a flat in Taunton. He's been a vital influence on me, particularly when things are going wrong. He is so strong, so convinced, that he fills you with fresh courage. Not many men are capable of that. We spend a lot of time together still; even during Test matches we will go out together in the evening or chat in our hotel rooms. On free days at home we might go shopping (people seem to find the sight of us buying Daz and those lemon things you squirt as incongruous as Mrs Thatcher playing bingo!), or we chat for hours, or watch television or a video. Sometimes we go to the ground for a game of snooker. Maybe we'll play golf. We never do much in the morning because it takes Viv hours to get himself ready. We spend a lot of time in the dressing-room, because there we can be ourselves. The lads know us, we aren't supposed to behave 'properly', and nothing we do or say will appear as headlines next day. It's like a sanctuary.

We do have a lot in common, being fellows who want to enjoy ourselves, and who will not be told what to do by anyone. We don't play public relations games, don't try to present ourselves as the nicest, smoothest couple in town. There are a lot of shallow creeps around who do that, men who apparently are just the sort of fellow every mum wants as her son. Some of these people are absolute shams – really insincere. Viv and I cannot be accused of that. Whatever else people say, they cannot accuse us of pretending to be sweet little boys. Images are nasty things – often they are simply the presentation of a surface. If it is newly painted then no one looks any deeper to see if there are cracks. And if your surface is a bit rough, who is it who will check to see if you aren't a little more substantial underneath?

On the field Viv composes himself. Every arrival is like the entry of the President. As he struts out you feel there should be a band striking up *Hail to the Chief*. This performance is his way of intimidating the bowlers. As he adjusts his cuffs, pats the top of his bat and stares at the bowler you can see the fielding team begin to wither. They can remember how nervous *they* felt, and yet here is this fellow preening himself as if he were a cat in a yard. He is showing them his contempt for everything that has gone before, all the weakness and defensive thinking, he is saying 'it is over'. Sometimes you can use this by challenging him – you can bowl wide, slip down a couple of maidens and peep at him as if to say, 'Come on then, big hero, where are the boundaries?' You can try to turn his bravado against himself.

Viv doesn't duck challenges. At Somerset we've seen three excellent overseas batsmen: Gavaskar, Crowe and Viv. Of these, Viv is the most explosive. Gavaskar is an 'I'm here for the day' fellow. When he settles in you wonder why he didn't bring a tent along. You feel that he is playing within himself; you feel as if he could murder you but he is determined to stay there all day. If Viv can destroy you in ten minutes he will, while Gavaskar gets in behind you and pushes you back down until you bowl a bad ball. It is as if he is saying, 'My, aren't you tired yet, Ian, but soon you will be. Then will come the day of reckoning.' He is patient. Crowe is a perfectionist. Whereas Gavaskar simply wants to pile on the runs, Crowe concentrates, hooding his eyes, staring down the pitch as if it is the only thing that matters. He wants to do everything right; every stroke must be just so. His score is interesting, but it is the means that he concentrates on. He wants to be elegant. Richards is the greatest player because he dominates mentally and physically. He doesn't care about anything else. I don't think Crowe will be great until he stops being a perfectionist and starts mutilating the bowlers. Technique, style, are only the means to an end, not the end itself. He must release himself so that he can bat with authority. Only then will he fulfil himself.

Richards's innings in the first one-day international at Old Trafford in 1984 – what was it, 189 not out out of 272? – was the best innings I've ever seen. There was not a ball anyone could bowl. Not a ball. He could step away and thrash it over cover or chip it over square leg. Remember we had everyone on the fence and Old Trafford is not a small ground. Willis bowled one ball to a full length on leg-stump and Richards smashed it over long-off off the back foot – the back foot! He did that at Hove once too. It was the sort of shot that goes further as the legend builds up. But I was there. He hit Snow, off the back foot, and hit the flats outside the ground. The ball didn't just carry over the sightscreen, it hit the flats! At Chelmsford once he cut a ball for six. You remember these shots by Viv because you cannot believe your eyes. He says there are fellows in the West Indies who are always cutting sixes! They don't seem to worry about their left elbows, they don't inhibit themselves. That is Viv's lesson to the magnificent technicians. Great players dominate, they don't wonder whether their knees are bending correctly.

If Viv has a weakness it is in touch shots. At golf he strikes the ball very well (though he does not use woods because they are not the same lengths as cricket bats) but around the green he is a little unreliable. His chips and his putts sometimes end up as far away as they began. He is not a fellow for delicate strokes. In cricket he loses his wicket caught sweeping and late cutting quite often, edging the ball to the slips or to square leg. He is not a master of these strokes, so that when he plays them the bowler feels he has a chance. Viv is at his best when he is hitting the ball through extra cover. If he is off-driving you know that his footwork is accurate and that he is not cramping himself. He says he is much more of a front-foot player than he used to be. In Antigua he used to use a short back-lift and crack everything past point, much as they say Everton Weekes used to do. Only upon his arrival in England, recognizing the need to adjust to movement, did he step forward and towards off-stump in the manner that is now his trademark. If Crowe, Gavaskar and Richards have something in common it is that they are all miraculous leg-side players. Wander over to leg and you are punished. I suspect most great batsmen have preferred to hit to leg, probably because there are so many more gaps over that side, and also because these masters move behind the ball every time. You do not see them reaching for a shot away from their bodies: everything is played under their chins.

These giants of the game are usually modest in private too. Maybe they feel a little more vulnerable than they care to show. Viv hates being called 'the world's greatest batsman'. He would not collect an award recently because the tannoy man kept calling him that. 'Why doesn't he use my name? Tell him my name is Vivian Richards. Why doesn't he call me that?' No one could understand him. But he wanted to be recognized as Viv, not by some boastful label: he isn't a brand of tea. He loves to cut a figure, Viv, but he isn't conceited at all off the field. On the contrary he tries to help lesser players as much as he can. Seeing him on the field, people assume that he is as proud as a peacock. In a way, I suppose cricket is too gentle for him; he ought to have been a boxer. He tried it for a while but it hurt his good looks! Most sportsmen, whether boxers or cricketers or darts players, are humble about themselves. They might reckon that they are the best in the world – which is why they *are* the best in the world – but they have also known failure, in a public way. Every great sportsman has had his bad times. Viv had to leave one ground in the West Indies by sneaking out of the back door of the pavilion – he was doing badly and the crowd were calling for his head. These things harden you, but they also teach you a little humility. The more you succeed the more your failures teach you and the more they toughen you.

Viv and I have struggled at times. Our struggles have been built up as epics so that every time we read a paper or switch on a television set, someone is saying something savage about us. These things harden the crust on the bread. They remind you how frail it all is, how little your past efforts will count if you fail today. In those times Viv and I sit at home and remember that he is the best batsman in the world and that I am the best all-rounder. In the end, it's as simple as that. In the end, we realize that we aren't the fellows who need to be worrying. We have learnt to take nothing for granted, but we have learnt too that it is the man who stays the longest who is the greatest. As they say, every dog has his day, but more of them last.

CHAPTER NINE

Two
Yorkshiremen

Botham has had a curious relationship with those two extraordinary Yorkshiremen, Brian Close and Geoffrey Boycott. He has many things in common with Close – he is married to a goddaughter of his – but very little in common with Sir Geoffrey, as his testimonial book was titled.

Close was Botham's first captain at Somerset. Ian was on the Lord's groundstaff in 1973 when a message arrived that he was to present himself at Taunton for a Sunday league game. Close had not heard of Botham – he seems rather vague about people, however precise he is about horses – but he selected him anyway. Ian was signed as a professional in 1974 and spent the next four years playing under Close's captaincy. It was a pity Close ever left because he was a man capable of imposing a measure of discipline upon the youngster.

Close was an unusual captain. He would arrive in the morning shortly before play began (the toss would often be late) and choose a team apparently at random. On the field he was relentlessly determined, clapping his hands if he thought someone was dozing, moving his fieldsman a yard this way, a foot that way, in accordance with some divine instruction. You never drifted when Close was captain. If the game was tight he'd start bellowing and charging around the field like a bull, committed to sorting the whole thing out himself. Sometimes, in his desperation, he'd wreak havoc by throwing inaccurately, or roaring ambiguous orders. (Once, chasing a ball, I heard him yell, 'Let it go, let it go'. I thought, 'Well, I can't throw it yet, I haven't caught up with the bloody thing'. Eventually I hurled the ball in, only to be confronted by Close who wanted to know why I hadn't allowed the ball to go to the boundary!) He was a gambler and an uncompromising competitor who expected intense efforts from his colleagues. He was also a man with a sense of fair play. Like Botham, he always walked if he knew he was out, and like Botham he could be reckless in his manoeuvres. He would follow his hunches without regret, and launch into long explanations of the extraordinary circumstances which had brought about their failure. Close never backed the wrong horse, only the wrong jockey.

There were many similarities between the furious old 'bald-headed bugger' and the strapping youngster. Close was aggressive, he had bulldog strength (he used to exercise as he cooked in a sauna), and he enjoyed the sensation of danger whether it be hooking fast bowlers, defying authority or driving fast cars. Botham and Close gamble, drink spirits and prefer the company of men. Not surprisingly, they used to fight all the time. Close had a stirring manner when roused – though in his twilight this was rare – and a few of the team used to retreat into the back room when they feared a storm. Botham did not. He would argue with his captain, cursing and defending himself with urgent arguments. A few hours later they'd be in the bar sharing a scotch, the best of friends. Close was a man strong enough, warm enough, determined enough, to match Botham. Odd that Close's wildest notions have brought him into violent conflict with the authorities, whereas Ian has escaped largely untouched. Perhaps Close's fights were too full of passion, too full of an overwhelming love of the game, whereas Ian's are more of a reflection of his combative character. Close is a cricketer to the core. Botham is an immense, forceful personality who happens to play cricket extraordinarily well.

Nor is it easy to imagine that Close, as a young man, was

as licentious as Ian. Botham can be like a character from an eighteenth century novel, hot-blooded, gallivanting, unquenchable. There is a bit of the puritan in Close, a sense that there is a proper way for a cricketer to do things. Close would never intentionally damage the image of the game. Ian cares not a jot for the old values.

Close's gambles, his huge errors, recollected the honest though foolish misjudgements of King Lear. And if Close ever stormed on to the dales it would not be in regret, it would be at the failure of the world to see that he was right. This inability to admit to a mistake is something he has in common with Botham. Ian's gambles, his sudden absurd selections, his improvized heaves, are not ideas merely taken too far. They are the result of daredevil risks, taken by a man trying to be inspired. Once Close, to the horror of his team, gave Richard Cooper and Mervyn Kitchen a bowl in a big game. Michael Procter was in. Neither man bowled much. Cooper did not even have a run-up. Nevertheless Kitchen dismissed Procter's partner, and in his solitary over Cooper had Procter dropped. A wild, inexplicable shot in the dark had nearly worked because behind it there worked a cricket brain half fanatical, half reckless. Ian's 'intuitions' rarely succeed because he lacks this essential grasp of the game. To him such a move is a huge, glorious joke which might come off. It was never any such thing to his former captain.

And yet Botham has been the greater cricketer, in a way the more substantial man. He has fulfilled his ability, whereas Close never proved himself to be a great Test cricketer. Botham has been England's mightiest player. Possibly Close was simply too rash, too bloody-minded, a man who never fully matured. Strangely, Ian's actions, in retrospect, appear far more acutely calculated than Close's. His boldness on the field is offset by an ability to gather friends. Ian has many social graces, and can be discreet and convincing when he needs to be. He has, perhaps, achieved more than Close because he played at a time when sport was beginning to tolerate the excesses of its heroes, and because he was more ruthlessly ambitious than his relation by marriage.

Botham's friendship with that other renowned Yorkshireman, Geoffrey Boycott, is prompted not so much by their characters as by their cricket. When Somerset and Yorkshire met at Headingley last year there was much mutual teasing. Botham observed that Boycott appeared to be losing his baldness, and asked if he was going to have yet another net. Boycott, who rarely talks to anyone except those he considers to be his equals, observed Botham's long, golden locks and wondered if they had been bleached by the sun. Evidently the two men liked each other, for it was as if they were renewing an old acquaintance. And yet their characters are so opposite. Boycott is extremely suspicious, living with barbed wire around his house. In Yorkshire he tolerates his unpopularity in the team, dedicating himself totally to his batting. Often he scores too slowly for the interests of his side, and then he has to survive the inquests which follow. He suffers the arguments of his opponents (few sit on the fence as far as Boycott is concerned) with a headstrong disdain which seems to spit in contempt at fellows who are not fit to wipe clean his boots daring to criticize his batting. It must be an icy, thankless life.

Boycott's laugh escapes from a corner of his mouth, as if he is reluctant to chuckle; Botham's laugh is hearty and open. Yet he explained that he has an affection for 'Boycs'. True, he ran him out deliberately in New Zealand when England were supposed to be pressing for quick runs, an act which won Botham the abiding friendship of most of the team, and certainly he has argued with Boycott occasionally – but he says he sympathizes with the man. He thinks that Boycott hides his finer qualities, dare not let them out because he has such tight control of his character. He is frustrated that Boycott, who has a dry wit, can be so pleasant and win friends only to

110

lose them immediately on some solitary, selfish act. Botham says that Boycott sees enemies everywhere – and feels he can only defend himself by accumulating runs, as a rich man gathers money to defeat a hostile world.

Sadly, this suspicion, with its barbed wire and its desperately protected tally, has cut Boycott off from his fellow players, it has distanced almost every player from him. Of course, his ostrich-like brethren believe this to be the inevitable condemnation of the excellent by the mediocre; they defend Boycott by pointing to his record and ask where we would all be without him. They'd be better off seeing the barbed wire and the lonely vigil of this master craftsman.

Ian's Story

Brian Close was captain throughout my early years with Somerset. He had arrived with the reputation of being a tough man and the idea was that he would improve the attitude of the older players and help to give the youngsters the early discipline they needed. In those days Somerset had a weak team and each man tended to play for his own statistics so that he could wave his figures to the committee at the end of the season. If your average was low you'd probably be sacked during the Weston Festival which was when these executions took place. It was really a matter of protecting your own career rather than trying to win a cup for your club. It is hard to avoid that in professional cricket. Players with wives and families are bound to look after themselves. If they don't they'll get some stick at home! There was one poor fellow who used to get home, open the door and his wife would say, 'Nipped back, did it?'

Close changed all this, or at least he helped to. He was used to winning things up in Yorkshire and expected the same at Somerset, though I imagine he found the people much more easygoing and the life much more fun. He shook things up, not so much by what he said as by his fighting qualities on the field. You wouldn't see him much in the bar at our hotels; he used to take his own kettle around and brew tea in the evenings when he wasn't drinking whisky with friends. But on the field he was totally involved. He used to frighten some of our players, they dare not make a mistake because he'd . . . well, I don't really know what they were frightened of, unless it was that he cursed a bit. They weren't used to it, I suppose. After years of gentle cricket, Close rampaged around the field, and some of our weaker players were never the same again. I don't blame Close for that, though he did tend to tar everyone with the same brush at times.

He was a funny man, though I'm not certain he realized it. Last summer he played in a benefit game at Taunton. Viv says he batted just the same as ever, with total determination, thrusting his head and his right foot forward, clouting full tosses. Viv bowled him out with a beauty. Afterwards apparently Close sat with his pads on for half an hour explaining to his team-mates what had gone wrong. After the game he walked into the Somerset dressing-room and explained his dismissal all over again. He had dropped a catch, too, and said that he had positioned himself perfectly but that the ball had fallen too quickly! He'd have you change the law of gravity by the end of the evening. If he was a fellow who ever considered he had made a mistake he would never have done as much as he did. In pre-season training he used to run around the field at an agonizingly slow pace, punching the air. We used to watch him because it was so hilarious. We thought if he went any slower he'd go backwards. He wasn't really a fellow for practice. He was a man for a match.

I suppose he destroyed himself against Benaud in 1961 and at Edgbaston with his delaying tactics. He still denies that he was cheating, but ironically the 29-overs-in-the-last-hour rule, which was brought in after Edgbaston, had been proposed a year earlier by D. B. Close. The incident cost him the England captaincy and ruined his career. But there was never any malice in him, nor any selfishness as a player. He was totally a team man. He was a bit like Churchill, asking no quarter and bearing no grudges.

We had lots of rows; bound to, two strong wills. The funniest incident of all – and even Close laughs about it now – was in a game against Surrey at Taunton. I think it was Geoff Howarth batting and I was bowling to him. He hit the ball and went for a quick single, changed his mind and was stuck in the middle of the pitch. I didn't know this, as I had slipped diving for the ball and had my back to what was going on, so I threw the ball and hit the stumps. Close then came up and gave me the biggest bollocking of all time – he shouted, 'You could have taken the bails off.' I replied, 'Well, I didn't know that; if no one shouts and tells me, how am I meant to know?' I can remember now the sight of Close storming up to me with his old, bald head, all the veins throbbing. I must admit that the stumps had gone all over Taunton. Another time, against Yorkshire, we collapsed to 80 for 7 one evening and I'd been out to a huge slog for 40. We were in terrible trouble and Close and I had a right to-do. Since I had hit 40, I couldn't understand why he was blaming me. He said it was a stupid irresponsible shot. Maybe it was, but it was just the sort of thing he'd do, a sudden crazy thing. He had a slog once in the last over before lunch, after playing magnificently for two tons. He stormed into the dressing-room and blamed his partner for not telling him what time lunch was! Another time he kept wicket when Jim Parks was injured during a cup game. We were in an almost invincible position when Parks left the field. Close took the gloves, found they didn't fit and decided to keep bare-handed: really heroic stuff, but we lost the match. He is an extraordinary man, lots of guts, tough as old boots and then, on the spur of the moment, rash.

My father-in-law, Jerry, took Close to pick up a sponsored car once. They found the garage mechanic giving the car a final shine, spit and polish. Closey said, 'Magnificent, lad, well done.' He got in the car, went round the roundabout straight into the back of a lorry, came back round to the garage and the bloke hadn't even put the duster away! Now that could only happen to Closey. He is magnificent, a great character.

Geoff Boycott could never be a successful captain of England, because he could never command the respect of the players. He is too self-centred. He proved that when he took over the side in Pakistan and New Zealand after Brearley was injured. I ran him out deliberately in New Zealand, in only my second Test match. There was the England captain blocking away when he was supposed to be going for runs. He was playing for his average and he was scoring too slowly, he didn't even want to declare on the last morning of the game. Bob Willis and I talked him into it and the game was over at 2.20. He was very quick to take the praise for it. That's what we didn't like.

Boycott has criticized every captain he has played under. He criticized me in one of his books, saying that I didn't consult him as captain. He implies that he made lots of suggestions and everyone ignored him and let him stew on the boundary. He hardly ever offered ideas. It was up to him to give help. It wasn't up to me to go to him as if he were an oracle. There were other experienced people and you didn't have to ask for an audience with them!

Geoff has never understood his own unpopularity. He couldn't see why we liked Brearley, he just thought Mike was a man born with a silver spoon who could not bat much and who had made it because of his background. He didn't think anything of Willis either. Boycott considers himself to be a master tactician, he believes he knows more about the game than anyone else, and that his origins have held him back. It is sad really, because he is a brilliant craftsman, an outstanding player in any era. He goes out, at his age, to face the bullets and yet he survives. Everyone wants to get him out more than any other batsman, yet still he scores runs. And then he'll go and do something daft like missing a game because he has followed the scores of a particular ground and he expects the pitch will be poor. He picks and chooses his games. He hardly ever seems to play on one or two wickets on the county circuit. He's such a good player, he's no need to hide. But, deep down, despite the curly-clipped arrogance he is terribly insecure. He needs those figures to *prove* that he is the best. His average is like a sword. He fights off the world by brandishing it. I feel sorry for Geoff; you wonder what he will take with him to the grave. All that unbeatable discipline, all those hard-earned, utterly dedicated, almost heroic innings and yet so little affection. He has sold his soul for his average – a sorry epitaph. Geoff is a flawed genius, a solitary man fighting a battle, hardening himself, drinking his tonic water, studying his figures. He must lead a terribly lonely life. I'm his last friend in the England team. I still enjoy his company. He can be funny, and I tease him, which he respects. Teasing is a mark of acceptance, like having a nickname.

But you cannot motivate a team with the word 'I'. Geoff cannot fool anyone; they know he's totally, almost insanely, selfish. He has been surrounded all his life by people who have said, 'Yes Geoffrey, yes Geoffrey', instead of someone turning around and saying, 'No you're wrong, Geoffrey'. It is a danger you face if you are a star. You're cut off and think everything turns around you. Nothing or no one else matters. The stupid thing is, the frustrating thing is, 'Boycs' can be really good fun. I've been out with him and we've had some good laughs and good times. We've had some hilarious rounds on golf courses. But then he'll undo all the good work in two minutes of total stupidity.

Boycott was sent home from India. His conduct was ridiculous; why do that? Why go and play golf when you're supposed to be dying in bed? Why not go out and see how the lads are doing? If he had come down and said, 'Look, I don't like it here – I'm going up to have a walk round the golf course, just to get my legs going', no one would have objected. He didn't, because he didn't think he had to. He'd broken Cowdrey's record, he was organizing a tour to South Africa, in secret, and he wasn't playing too well. His mind was twisted – he couldn't see things straight.

He is a great player, but what use is that if you can't enjoy it? He thinks the world is against him, because he's from Yorkshire, because he didn't go to a public school, because he's honest and so many people around him tell him he's right. He's a god to them. There's no prejudice against Boycott, just an accurate assessment of his character. Really his problem is that people are not blind to his faults. Only people who do not understand the game praise him. Whenever have you heard a present player say he's a good man to have in a team? His defenders say this is envy, that Geoff scores more runs than anyone else, so people want to drag him down. But you never hear the same condemnation of Amiss, or Lamb, or Robinson. They will respond to the needs of their team: Boycott will not. Cricket is a team game. In the end, it's as simple as that.

CHAPTER TEN

The All-Rounders

In September 1984, a few days after Nottinghamshire had failed to win the championship at Taunton, the most esteemed all-rounders in the world gathered there to compete for the day, for the Silk Cut Trophy. It was an odd idea. Nothing much can be settled on a wind-swept autumnal afternoon at the end of the season. Still, it brought together Botham's rival all-rounders and presented a fine opportunity to compare the men. I'd hoped to discuss these rivals with Ian, to see if he had anything illuminating to say about them. He did not. Throughout the day he was curiously muted, as if missing the fellowship of his team. He wanted to win, but in the dressing-room, surrounded by these other national heroes, he was ill at ease. At times he still feels like a county cricketer in a big bad world. Without his mates around him, he feels naked.

His reticence was probably not a sign of humility. Ian says he is the best all-rounder in the world. He says he has scored thirteen Test hundreds while none of his supposed rivals has scored more than three. But he is sensitive to Sobers's comment that you cannot be great if your batting average is 15 and your bowling average 50 against the West Indies. He felt that at Lord's in 1983, when he defied Cowans, Daniel and Williams to win a game for his team; during the 1984 Test series when he and Lamb were easily the best England batsmen; and in 1985, when he cracked bumper after bumper from Marshall off his eyebrows, he proved his status against the greatest bowlers. He feels that none of the others measure up to him, that none of those criticisms of his weaknesses against fast bowling is tenable. He believes these things but will not say them. He suggested only that I watch the cricket on that uneasy Saturday, read the career records of the players, and draw my own conclusions: so I did.

Clive Rice won the day, a victory repeated a year later at Arundel, because he studied the rules, realized that if he did not lose his wicket and could take a couple himself he could hardly be beaten. Botham finished third, largely because his batting partner ran him out. Also Rice took more wickets than anyone else, ironically because, as the worst bowler, he was the man to be punished. Besides which Marshall, showing his contempt for the contest, swiped and lost his wicket to Rice three times.

Rice has never played Test cricket, never experienced its peculiar pressures, and so he cannot really be compared to the others. His compatriots, bustling Barlow and imperious Procter, were at least able to play in a few internationals before the shutters went up. Rice is condemned to being a minor cricketer who will, sadly, be forgotten by history. He can be judged only by what he has done, not by what might have been. In first-class cricket Rice has scored over 20,000 runs (average 40) and taken some 750 wickets at about 22 apiece. In the winter of 1984–85 he finished top of the Currie Cup batting averages, in front of Pollock, Kirsten and Fotheringham. These are impressive statistics, the most impressive of those present that day at Taunton especially as Rice has also captained Nottinghamshire and Transvaal with success. Last winter (1985–86) he led South Africa to victory over Kim Hughes's rebel Australians. In the one-day games (won 4–2 by South Africa) he was voted man of the series. In county cricket he has one advantage over the others – it is the highest level he can reach and so he approaches it with fierce dedication. Others are sometimes tempted to regard a county game much as a test pilot might regard a trip in a Mosquito.

Despite his Silk Cut victories, Rice is not quite an all-rounder these days. For several seasons a neck injury has forced him to bowl at medium pace. He had been a hostile fast bowler who charged in, head down, from a short run, leaning back before hurling himself at the batsman. He was a bowler who, as Gooch once said of Pascoe, 'favoured the short-pitched delivery'. He'd pound the middle of the pitch, flinging the ball at the batsman's throat. By way of variety he would pitch the ball up, trying to defeat any timid batsman who trod pessimistically towards his stumps. Rice hunted those who flinched, launching himself at them until they were dismissed. He never said much, being one of those cautious, apparently slow-thinking South Africans, but he played his cricket with great fervour.

Of the all-rounders Rice is the most disciplined, the most controlled. Oddly this might explain why in this company he may be the least. The others stretch into avenues beyond orthodoxy; Rice appears less imaginative, less gifted. He cannot match Botham's flair; his technique is sound but he is restricted by it whereas Botham uses his superb skills as a foundation for adventure. Nevertheless he is a magnificent cricketer and a proud captain. Though he *is* a fine cricketer, he is not a truly great all-rounder in my opinion.

Malcolm Marshall is an unorthodox number eight rather than a feared number six. He would not be selected for the West Indies as a batsman – he would not even be chosen by Barbados or Hampshire were it not for his blistering bowling. In 36 Test matches his average is 17 and he has not scored a century. In first-class cricket he has hit 4,000 runs at an average of 21. These are moderate figures. Not that Marshall minds. When he bats in county cricket he usually resembles a conductor flourishing his baton through a particularly lively waltz. But Marshall's batting is improving. When he arrived in England he used to swish about like a fish on the end of a hook. This approach did not succeed, so the West Indian decided to adopt the cautious, canny technique of English batsmen, who found their game upon the supposition that every ball is to be mistrusted, and a half-volley is probably a trap. West Indians are more used to clobbering the ball if it is within reach. From slip Viv Richards would call, 'Oh man, you are not an Englishman. Where have all the shots gone?' Eventually Marshall worked out a method which put him with the all-rounders in the Hampshire batting order.

In any event Marshall's prowess, or lack of it, with the bat is irrelevant beside his vicious pace with the ball. Somerset's groundsman, Gordon Prosser, says that Marshall is the fastest bowler he has seen since Lindwall and adds that he might even have the edge on the great Australian. His approach is like a runaway train, a hurtling, frantic rush which, despite its speed, loses neither rhythm nor fluency. Marshall's extraordinary pace is produced not by strength (he stands 5 feet 11 inches tall and weighs 12 stone) but by a fast arm and a late snap of the wrist. He is, too, a dedicated and unstinting cricketer who commits himself to his team in every game. Marshall is supreme as a fast bowler; he knows it, and means to stay supreme as long as he can.

Richard Hadlee resembles a rickety church steeple, solemn, silent, almost sombre; he is a forbidding man who expects high standards of himself. Alone amongst the current all-rounders he does not hide his reliance upon statistics, nor his determination to improve them. In 1984 Hadlee decided to try to do the double of 1,000 runs and 100 wickets, a target not achieved by anyone since Fred Titmus in 1967. Hadlee carried a book around with him in which he recorded every performance, adding his tally as he went from game to game. He worked out how many runs and wickets he needed at every stage of the season. He reached the double and his team missed the championship by a hit.

He is a methodical man, this lean, intense fast bowler from New Zealand. He stands apart from his team, rarely says much in the dressing-room, preferring to concentrate upon his own game. During a day's play – every day's play – he paces himself, not letting his emotions goad him into sudden, draining bursts. His opening spell will be short, and will rely more upon movement and variation than destructive pace. He does not want to wear himself out, for the day, for the season, in hot-headed assault. In mid-morning he'll return for a second brief burst, still rarely reaching full blast. After lunch he will launch a third attack before retiring to slip to be roused only when the tail is exposed. Then, suddenly, he will bowl very fast, determined to add the tail to his haul. Sometimes this tight, disciplined approach infuriates his team-mates, who accuse him of lacking the wholehearted gusto which cricketers expect of each other. Hadlee is sensitive to the charge – which is heard more in New Zealand than in Nottingham. He may have done the double for himself, but that is simply how he motivates himself, and it did help the team too. Few outstanding cricketers perform with the consistency of Hadlee, however willing they appear.

The New Zealander is open about his use of figures as a way of disciplining his game. Like Boycott, he collects statistics rather more obviously than most cricketers but, unlike Boycott, his team rarely suffers from his single-mindedness. Hadlee's character contrasts dramatically with Botham's. Ian tends to regard Hadlee as a bit of a *prima donna*, perhaps too as rather a drip. Hadlee, one suspects, finds Botham's vulgarity hard to tolerate. Their duel began in 1977 when Botham hooked Hadlee and was caught on the boundary as England sank to embarrassing defeat in New Zealand. It is a duel that has lasted for eight years, with victories on both sides.

Hadlee is a superb bowler, more skilful than Marshall though not as fast. Like a representative of the Inland Revenue Hadlee exacts everything on offer. With a high arm and a wrist which breaks as sharply as Marshall's, he is able to lift the ball from dozing pitches. Steep bounce is vital to bowlers of every pace. Without it edges do not carry, batsmen can use bat and pad to kill the ball and movement is more easily countered. At Somerset Tom Cartwright's greatest quality was the life he imparted to the ball. He relied upon his bounce as much as his accuracy and command over cut.

In Test matches Hadlee has taken 266 wickets at an average of 24, superb statistics especially considering the want of support. His batting average is only 25 (2,088 runs) and he has struck only one century. In the last three years his batting has improved because he is so excellent a bowler that he can go for his shots with impunity. He is lean, upright and swings his bat, without Botham's savagery but with a long, clean sweep. Hadlee's assaults have tended to lead to swift seventies rather than magnificent hundreds. He has not turned the course of Test matches often enough to be regarded other than as a great bowler who is a threat at the crease.

Kapil Dev Nikhaj of Punjab University and Imran Khan Niazi of Aitchison College, Lahore, and Oxford, remain as Botham's only true challengers now that Michael Procter has retired. Kapil is the youngest player to take 100 Test wickets (he was 21 according to his Indian birth certificate) and the youngest to pass 1,000 Test runs. Both times he broke Ian Botham's record. Kapil has scored 2,788 runs (average 30) and taken 258 wickers (average 28) in Test cricket, figures only slightly less impressive than the Englishman's. He is a gifted, nonchalant cricketer but probably isn't a match for Botham.

Kapil bowls in a similar style, though his swingers are more silky, more effervescent, than Botham's thunderous deliveries. The Indian relies more upon wit than his bulldozing rival. But like Botham, Kapil Dev prefers to work for his wickets, bowling in long spells, willing to risk punishment for the chance of a breakthrough. He is a brave, inviting bowler though, as with Botham, years of hard work on sweltering days has stolen a little of his nip. Kapil and Botham depend for their effect upon a spirit which bears no denial. They have their differences, though. Botham is raw, strong, all blood and sweat. Kapil is sleek, wiry, deceptive.

As captain Kapil has led his country to a World Cup victory (in 1983) though his reign has been dogged by controversy. Each man was appointed captain because of his heroic qualities; the selectors had an image of a chap riding a white horse, sword in hand, shouting 'Charge!' It did not prove so simple. The troops were too sceptical. Nevertheless, Kapil has won a World Cup, an experience he shares with only Clive Hubert Lloyd. His catching of Richards in the final was typically bold, typically without hesitation, a thirty-yard sprint with all India holding its breath. Still more significantly Kapil rescued his team from 17 for 5 against Zimbabwe with a staggering and unbeaten 175, another phoenix from the ashes.

A year later, a dark year in which the West Indies avenged that World Cup defeat, and Kapil was back on the shelf, to rise again only when Gavaskar resigned on winning the World Championship of Cricket in Australia. Certainly Kapil was a more mature, more respected captain in 1986, and led India to a comfortable two-nil series win over England. Still Kapil is curiously slow to move in for the kill. Like Botham he lacks a certain acumen, and, also like Botham, he is probably too reluctant to speak to his team as its boss rather than as one of the boys.

Yet Kapil is not Botham. He cannot destroy so totally. There is something faintly flimsy about the Haryana Hurricane, something suspiciously light about him. In his *Who's Who* entry (the *Cricketers' Who's Who* that is) he reveals that Test cricket should be 'on a plane above all other games, a beautiful sport'. People have expressed similar sentiments about war, but cricketers are usually more sceptical. Botham certainly is – he does not regard himself as a cricketer of enchantment.

Spectators think Botham could bat forever if only the blasted fellow would keep his head down. Kapil has scored only three Test centuries, one of them in a game long condemned to a draw. He has passed 50 eighteen times in Test matches for his three tons. Botham has passed 50 thirty-one times and carried on to three figures on thirteen occasions. In 1984–85 with his team in trouble, Kapil swiped at Pocock's every ball and was caught at mid-off after hitting a six. He was dropped for the next game.

Imran Khan did not play in the all-rounders' competition at Taunton in 1984, and only returned to cricket as an all-rounder in January 1985, after two years suffering from fractured shins (apparently the X-rays show something of a jigsaw). He is a strong, imperious man, proud of his nation, proud of himself. He has the air of a patrician in contrast to Botham's determinedly plebeian image. Imran is a quiet, thoughtful man who says he does not eat pig meat, drinks three-and-a-half pints of milk a day, and wears a verse from the Koran around his neck. Though not as devout a Moslem as his cousin Majid, Imran is evidently a man of firm principle.

In Test cricket Imran has scored 2,023 runs (average 31) and reached his hundred twice. His bowling is more impressive, 232 wickets at an average of 23. Imran has represented Pakistan as a batsman/captain, unable to bowl, to his immense frustration. His batting is orthodox, though he can lift an off-drive over extra cover. Rather like Hadlee, Imran has only recently been regarded as a serious Test batsman. Nor has he changed the course of a Test match in a session as has Botham. Imran's ambitions are less dramatic. He bats with a sense of duty, a sense of his team's situation, whereas Botham attacks without inhibition whatever the score. Imran remains an awesome athlete, a glorious fast bowler and a useful batsman in Test cricket.

Lest it be argued that Botham, though a more substantial batsman, is not nearly as good a bowler as these men, it ought to be observed that he has taken 5 wickets in a Test innings no less than twenty-six times. None of the others can match that. No, for all Botham's flaws, he stands alone as an all-rounder, to the supreme irritation of those of solemn attitude.

CHAPTER ELEVEN

In The Papers

A few years ago Ian Botham was fat, a fact he was able to hide from himself until he saw some photos. Our papers, scarcely the refuge of sober, articulate, celibate or public-spirited men, were scandalized. They launched a campaign concentrating upon Botham's swollen waistline. Very quickly the interest deteriorated to a desperate scrounging for titbits, undertaken by gentlemen from the more dramatic papers. Some arrived in Bristol, not to describe the game but to pinch the menu-cards. These cards, speaking of pork chops and ice-cream, were printed next day. Few Somerset players bothered with lunch for it was too hot and we were fielding. A few nibbled at a salad. Botham dozed in the dressing-room, sipping a cup of tea. Not to be deterred, the popular press then sent its agents to Epworth where they interviewed Botham's butcher and baker (neither said anything).

It is shameful, this unkind light which is cast over the life of top sportsmen. Squalid stories are written in the name of freedom of the press. Botham's reaction to such enquiries has been furious. He considers this fascination with his affairs to be grotesque, and cannot understand why editors demand these bizarre stories. His fury has led him to reject every journalist, a rejection that is unfair besides being ill-advised. Botham writes for one of the worst offenders – *The Sun* – and is very well paid to do so. If he is aggrieved at his treatment

126

by the papers then he ought not to lend his name to any of them.

The dispute shows neither side in a particularly good light. Botham and some other England players retreat from all journalists, which is not just, though even those with integrity cannot expect to be entirely trusted if their profession is tainted. Too many of them have broken the line between legitimate criticism and personal abuse. Too many of them, searching for headlines, fail to sympathize with the struggling cricketer or the defeated team. It is cosy to sit in the stands and to judge, easy to sit with mates in the press box and develop, hardly realizing it, a collective view of the state of English cricket or the size of Botham's tummy or whatever.

On the other hand, leading cricketers are too sensitive. They are not immune from criticism. Politicians, novelists, singers, bishops are not beyond criticism and neither are sportsmen. There is a tendency in cricket to regard the written word as a branch of public relations.

Some sportsmen seem to believe all criticism to be a sign of personal hostility. I found this difficult to understand when I joined Somerset from Cambridge University. Being used to sharp debate, I was surprised at the concern professional cricketers felt at the slightest dissent. They did not distinguish between an intellectual though violent argument and personal animosity. If you had a row with someone then you didn't like them, whether the subject of the row was bombs or run-outs.

Ian is proud that he has never attacked a fellow player in print. He gives short shrift to those who do. He expects English papers to support the English team rather as *Tribune* supports Labour. Naively, and unjustly, he views criticism as disloyalty. Very often papers have written accurate but unpleasant things about Ian. His anger is not lessened by considerations of truth. He hates the burrowing away the personal side of his life, which he says is no one's business but his own. He is not much impressed by fair points about his cricket. He thinks writers forget his best efforts and remember only his mistakes.

Cricketers often tend to distance themselves from journalists because they suspect them to be parasites. This is not fair either. It is usually easier, though often much less fun, to describe something rather than to do it. But one of cricket's proudest boasts is that it has been written about by gifted writers in an inspiring manner. The game has attracted many people of sensitive temperament and literary flair. It has given us men of humanity and judgement who have been able to capture the game for us, to bring it to life for us. A cricketer and a cricket writer are not like author and critic, they are more like Gilbert and Sullivan. Cricket would in a way be much less without its best authors. It is not for the player to deny the writer his ability to include in his report the good things and the bad.

Ian does over-react towards the press, an over-reaction born of some admittedly appalling activities by a few papers. Nevertheless his fame owes much to publicity, and if his qualities are to be trumpeted to the nation he cannot suppose that his failings will be hidden. It would be nice, though, if the tabloids were more careful as to what they print. A part of Botham's mistrust lies in the ineffectiveness of a retraction. Once a statement appears in black and white, the damage is done.

Botham's other area of extreme sensitivity is in his relationship with the forces of law and order. He believes that investigating journalists have worked with the police in an effort to destroy his reputation. He has been charged with assault and several times convicted of speeding. More recently, and far more damagingly, he has pleaded guilty to possessing cannabis. He believes that some accusations are the result of an effort to prick his vanity, to bring down the reckless, ambitious and unapologetic young man. He says he has not changed since he was nineteen (which is true) and argues that people are envious and trying to hurt him.

There is something in what he says. Since his image changed from knight in shining armour to notorious bandit, his conduct has been regarded differently. His image has changed; his youthful vigour is now perceived as nasty arrogance. The drug conviction was a part of this change. Would the police have raided someone else's house on New Year's Day? Was this the only party in England at which there might have been drugs? Botham's house was raided because he has been naughty, because his reputation has been dragged through gutters, because people were not prepared to turn a blind eye. It would be more generous if Ian was more often taken as a whole – if the odd punch, the odd extreme of behaviour was seen to be a part of the character of a man who has lifted English cricket, and a part to be understood. In a land in which Boycott's coldness can be cherished, Botham's warmth can surely be endured.

Ian was desperately hurt by the drug investigations, and will tolerate no teasing or joking on this subject. He was appalled that youngsters might imagine him to be some sort of drug addict. He wants to be a hero; he doesn't mind the larger-than-life stories about drink or crashing cars or late nights. He wants to be respected by the young, though not necessarily respectable in the eyes of the old. He had not thought himself to be anything other than a high-spirited fellow, much put upon. The revelations about drugs outraged him, and when he returned from Pakistan he would not discuss the matter with anyone. His wife remembers that he seemed harder, more ruthless, more self-contained. It was as if he were a pop star who had realized that people were not going to buy his records any more.

Botham's has been a turbulent career. Cricketers do not belong on the front pages of newspapers, especially if they are there for reasons beyond their skills on the field. He is not so much a creation of the press, not so much a Frankenstein, as a man prone to outrage whose name can sell newspapers, and who is seized upon for that purpose.

Ian's Story

The modern cricketer, in the week of a Test match, gets more media coverage than W. G. Grace got in the whole of his playing days. W. 'G. Grace isn't mentioned in history books, he wasn't on television or video. These days you are so much more exposed.

People write differently now, because the papers are in competition with each other for a story. If it isn't bingo or the royal family, it's Botham's latest escapade. The reporters don't investigate properly because there isn't time. They hear a rumour, are terrified that someone else will hear it, and so bang it on to the front page and smile to themselves if their rivals have missed it. One up for the lads, that's how it works. There isn't a lot of dignity involved. They worry later about being sued for libel, or about hurting some innocent party. People don't matter beside the search for a story. Writers with principles get left behind.

During the Yorkshire Ripper case, journalists were charging around destroying the lives of relatives by thrusting exclusive contracts in their faces. Their conduct was utterly disgusting, without respect, without sympathy, without humanity. It isn't the journalists' fault, it is the editors and the owners who put pressure on them. After years on the front pages I have no respect whatsoever for our papers. Nothing you see described ever bears any resemblance to what happened. You cannot recognize the same incident. Rodney Hogg and I were supposed to have had a fight once, on New Year's Eve. Nothing happened. We didn't. People said, 'Oh well, he's denying it, but there's no smoke without fire'. That is the trouble. A story can be printed and it will be believed simply because it *is* in print.

Cricketers now aren't cricketers at all any more, not if they are internationals. They are interesting characters who, suddenly, lead their lives in public. They are not anonymous from 6.30 until the next morning. Anything, any whisper,

130

about them is printed. Editors used to say they were not interested in what Keith Miller did, whether he turned up in his top hat and tails, or whether someone threw a jug of water over a maharajah. Cricket writers reported the game and then joined the lads in the bar for a pint. This trust has been betrayed. News reporters are now sent on tour, and some journalists are told to unearth every scandal they can. Scandals are front page news: centuries are a paragraph just above *Hagar the Horrible* on the back page.

In 1985 I was in trouble for cursing during a Test match against Australia. How on earth can you get into trouble for cursing during a Test match? You'd never get a team on the field! Once, such things would have been ignored with a shrug and a smile. The drama of an over, bouncers, catches, no-balls, warnings, lbw appeals, could have filled a report, instead of which some maiden-aunt in Eastbourne who can lip-read is found to say that I swore. It is a matter of emphasis. That one moment was built up, headlines were written, and disciplinary committees met. Such moments create the image of Botham and the image of cricket. This is irresponsible reporting.

Yet, whatever my faults, bad conduct on the field is not amongst them. I've never bumped into an umpire, never kicked over a stump, never thrown a bat, never argued with an opponent, never run anyone out unfairly, never claimed a catch that did not carry. I'm an honest cricketer. So are most other cricketers, a couple of villains apart.

Once a 'baddy' is established, a witch hunt begins. Editors sit in their offices and ask, 'Any good stories about Botham this morning?' People think this is fine until it happens to them. Some papers will tell their reporters to go to any lengths for a story. Once we were having a meeting in a tent at Weston-super-Mare a couple of years ago discussing contracts, a very private and important meeting. In walks this fellow from the *Daily Mail* to say that his paper was printing some story about England cricketers drinking heavily in pubs dur-

131

ing a Test match. He wanted a statement. He just strolled in, announced his idiotic story and demanded a comment which he could then twist. Who the hell is interested in whether I had a few pints of an evening? It was an incredibly rude thing to do, too.

I don't believe sportsmen are any different now from the way they have always been. They are presented in a different way, that is all. Actually I suspect that for the most part we are a nicer lot altogether. There are some terrific men playing cricket for England, really outstanding characters, fellows worth ten times as much as the cheap snakes who condemn them, not as cricketers but as people.

I live my life in the public arena, more so even than the Prime Minister. In the summer of 1985 she went on holiday for a fortnight to Austria, and nothing was heard of her. My holidays are public property. They want to know what I'm up to every hour of every day just in case, just in case. You may say that this interest has helped me to buy my house, because my fame, my notoriety, has brought me lots of money. Some people suggest that I deliberately create incidents so that I will be on the front pages. I heard it said that my supposed row with Alan Whitehead was prompted by my agent's advice to stage a stunt. This is outrageous and insulting. I'm no Cassius Clay. I crashed two Saabs once, and this was the first item on the television news and the front pages next day: Botham the reckless driver. Saab were delighted because they had never enjoyed so much free publicity! But I'd been driving Saabs around that race-track for years. I enjoy it. No one mentioned that. It wasn't a stunt. Actually I crashed twice on the same corner! The second time the managing director was with me in the car. He thought he'd be safe as I'd be more careful after the first accident. That was an error of judgement! If something goes wrong I jump back in and do it again.

I'm sorry that cricketers are presented in such a damning way. It is unfair. I think a lot of journalists regret it too – none

132

of them wanted to write about the business in Pakistan – they are trapped in a web of hard selling. What we need is a Press Council which has the guts to demand fair play. Our papers – our tabloids – are not the best papers in the world, they are the worst.

I've had my ups and downs with the police too. Once you have a reputation it is hard to lose it. People treat you differently; they expect trouble and start looking under stones for it. It is probably the same in a classroom. You have a kid who is supposed to be a right villain, and you watch him closely. Maybe he's not really any worse than the others, just a little less discreet. Insincerity, meanness, unkindness are faults too, maybe worse faults than a punch in a pub; but they are less dramatic, harder to write angry articles about.

I've been caught speeding a few times. It's not a thing I do consciously. I don't go up the motorway too fast in the hope of being caught: far from it. More often than not I'm caught when I'm going home. Once I was chased up the motorway for five miles; I was heading for my first Test match and was hardly aware of what I was doing. The policeman said it was the best chase he'd had in his life! He said he really enjoyed it, and he was sorry he had to book me. It used to be like that. Another time a blue light flashed in the car behind so I pulled over, cursing that I'd been caught again. I wound down the window and the constable asked for my autograph! That was all he wanted. I was on my way to Lord's and he said, 'Good luck tomorrow'.

Sadly things are different now. It is as if the word has gone round to 'nail Botham'. I was charged with doing 125 mph once. I thought, 'Well, that's strange, this car will only do 116'. The case was thrown out. A second time I was driving home after leaving Taunton at nine at night. If I hadn't hurried I'd never have reached home. Next day the papers said I'd told the policeman, 'You can't touch me, I'm Ian Botham'. In court the policeman repeated this. I'd no idea he'd do that. He had asked my name and I had said, 'My name is Ian Botham'. He asked where I was going and I told him. He stood up in court and made these simple statements sound awful . . . I wanted to do something about it but my wife said there was no point since the damage had been done.

My life is scrutinized now for faults. George Best suffered for the same reason. His infidelities, his drinking sessions were all reported. Do you suppose no other Manchester United player ever did such things? He was presented as a bad boy, while the others were saints. Yet Best was the fellow who would do things for charity. He was utterly harmless. Some of the others screwed every penny they could from appearances at charity functions. They were more careful than Best, but they lacked his qualities too. If you keep your hands clean, or appear to do so, you are treated kindly even if you never do a thing for anyone.

I have handled things badly at times I know, and played into the papers' hands. I'm not whiter than white – far from it. Still, if I'm in a club and there is a fight you will see headlines saying 'Botham in bar brawl', irrespective of whether I was trying to stop the fight or joining in. We had a battle years ago when some of the Hampshire lads went with me to a benefit do at Taunton soccer club. Some idiots were fooling around and they fell on to the table next to me. For some reason a fracas began and suddenly one of their lads was being beaten up, so I lent him a hand and we left. Next morning the headlines are blazing. Mind you, two big blokes turned up at lunchtime and said they wanted to see me behind the old pavilion. As it turned out they wanted to apologize for getting me into trouble! That was good of them. As a matter of fact, they were in a bit of a state, too, which pleased me a bit – they were enormous blokes!

As far as I'm concerned, if the papers want to send a news reporter to England's hotel to sit in the foyer to see when the players go to bed, they can. It is like a declaration of war. They are not sympathizers who understand our lives, or remember their own mistakes and avoid bringing ours into the open. They are not trustworthy and so they cannot expect anything from me. It doesn't matter what I say, they print what they choose. So why should I help them?

CHAPTER TWELVE

Let Tomorrow
Worry About Itself

Ian Botham is an odd, contradictory sort of hero. He is the fellow who can eat three Shredded Wheat, the fellow who was only a reserve at Scunthorpe and nevertheless advertized football boots. He is the man who rescued England, the man who hits sixes and catches blinders. And yet he has been charged with a variety of crimes, has been involved in brawls, and has been rude to spectators. After his extraordinary effort in the Jubilee Test match Botham was a hero in India; whereas after his fight with Chappell and his imagined buffeting of Hogg, he is a villain in Australia. It is all very confusing.

Ian wants to appear as he sees himself, as a bit of a ruffian, a bloke who is game for a laugh. He sees himself as an ordinary man with ordinary tastes. But he knows he is a star too, so to the snooker and the beer are added less robust habits. He *wants* to be *Roy of the Rovers*, the hero who rescues lost causes; he does not want to be Ned Kelly. But he is not a stable, predictable hero. His followers gasp at his disasters, shudder at his bouts of failure and roar at his sudden brilliance. Botham is not a cold man who denies his emotions and conquers his instincts. Sportsmen like Laver, Davis, Watson, Piggott, Lauda and Borg do not torment their followers, or themselves, as he does; they are consistent – but in their very level-headedness perhaps a little warmth is lost. You do not watch them with your stomach churning, wondering whether they will reach too far, and destroy themselves with rash moves.

Botham is a man of intuition and instinct, one of those who cannot resist trying the more acute angle or the most difficult challenge. He is a cricketer of mood, at his best passionate, at his worst erratic. Other sportsmen whose passionate spirit contrasts with the calculation of colder men include Ali, Best, Ballesteros, Higgins, Nastase, Richards, Hoad – all have a fallibility in common, the lurking threat of self-destruction. These are men who rely upon provocation to stir the spirit. They can be morose too, with a tendency to sulk; they are men who submit to, rather than discipline, their emotions. With this mixture of vulnerability and brilliance they carry with them their supporters. Botham is like that. He is a culprit whom it is hard to condemn: he can be forgiven almost any-thing because he offers so much, and because he didn't really mean it anyway. He is a fellow you can live neither with nor without.

Many of sport's epic struggles have been battles between the hot and the cold – Ballesteros versus Watson, Higgins versus Davis, Hoad versus Laver – contests between admirable men who apply their strength to protect their weaknesses, and men who want to enchant, to destroy, to dazzle. Botham follows the fortunes of Ballesteros and Higgins, frequently betting on them, especially if they are in a bad trot. He realizes they, like him, are fellows who need to be roused, he knows that they are ill at ease when they are expected to do well. He admits himself that he enjoys returning to his peak just as he is being most roundly chastised. At times it seems as if he encourages his losses of form by wilful neglect of technique and physique. He has allowed himself to put on weight, swung recklessly, even deliberately tempted the fates by repeating an idiotic stroke which had previously brought about his downfall. It is not entirely conscious, this streak of self-destruction. It is as if Botham senses he must turn the tide of expectation lest it hinder his freedom to indulge his wildest notions. So much has been expected from him for so long. He has carried the burden of his national team since 1977 and yet he has never been a reliable cricketer. He does not *want* to be a reliable cricketer. It is the thrill of the dramatic rescues, the sudden changes of fortune, which intoxicate Botham.

And what of the wife who has to stay at home, who has to put up with this turbulent cricketer? Kathy and Ian married in 1976 when Ian was still an unknown youngster. At the time he was in debt to most of us ('Lend me a fiver till the weekend, will you?') and when he wasn't chasing Kathy he was down at the pub accepting any challenge of any sort. He could drink faster and punch harder and eat more prodigiously than anyone else.

Kathy didn't expect her lean, ruggedly handsome husband to hurtle to the top quite so quickly and his notoriety has presented difficulties to her and to their children, Sarah, Liam and Rebecca. They never quite know if their dad is Richard the Lionheart, Henry VIII or Richard III (in the Elizabethan versions). With Ian so much in demand it has been left to Kathy to bring up the children, a difficult task for they are as strong-willed as their father. Liam is Ian's shadow. He used to cry whenever Ian climbed into his car to leave for a few days, but he is used to it now and makes sure that when his dad is home he sees plenty of him. He is a frequent visitor to the Somerset dressing-room and often plays cricket on the field in the breaks.

It cannot be easy living with Ian; he is easily bored and, as a star, tends to expect everything to revolve around him. Rather like a warrior returning from a battle, at home Ian wants to put his feet up, to be waited on and to relax; naturally his family, deprived of his company for weeks, have all sorts of plans for him. His brief spells at home are his chance to unwind and his family's chance to get him to mow the grass, to visit friends, to go on picnics and to fish.

It is probably just as well the Bothams live away from the cricket. Too often, when she was in Somerset, Kathy had to suffer the comments of spectators who did not recognize her. She is wise to live in the north, surrounded by relations and friends. It was a pity that they had to leave Epworth, though.

Ian has a fierce temper which at times he cannot curb, and he is immensely strong. He is even a little afraid of himself. In 1985 he scrapped once in the dressing-room, over some fairly trivial argument, with Richard Ollis, a young batsman and a friend of his. Ollis later observed that Ian's eyes had gone quite black, and that he was terrified. I have seen Viv Richards do the same, cornering someone who had given offence and tearing into him, his eyes blazing.

Ian's temper is vital to his triumph as a cricketer, though. It is said that Sobers was really angry only twice in his career – once when Bill Lawry did not enforce a follow-on and set the West Indies over 700 to win. Sobers did not believe this was the way to play cricket and marched out to smash a hundred. The other time was during the Rest of the World tour of Australia in 1971. One night Sobers was upset by some private matter; next day he thrashed his way to 254. Botham's passion is much nearer to the surface than that; he is a far less gentle individual. He can unleash himself more easily, and when this occurs on a cricket field the result is spectacular. Against Australia in 1981 he won a Test match with a spell of 5 for 1. It was a burst of bowling that could not be resisted. The balls were straight, there was nothing special about them. It was Botham who, with a spirit and a will not to be resisted, demolished the batsmen. He can produce a power which brooks no argument. This is not merely aggression, but the mixture of fear and authority created by a hawk as it gazes upon a thrush: I'm going to get you: don't stand in my way. It is a primeval message.

To protect him from himself, Ian employs Andy Withers, a gentle buffalo of a man who has been a friend of Ian's for years. Andy absorbs Ian's temper, those fierce moments which are either understandable reactions to pressure, or the tantrums of a *prima donna*, depending upon your view. He is a secretary who persuades Ian to fulfil his obligations, who replies to his letters and who helps to arrange meetings and other business matters which interest Botham very little. Most important of all Andy is a companion. Everywhere Ian goes he takes Andy, so that he never enters a pub, or a shop, or a nightclub alone. This is not only to 'keep the wallies at bay', it is also to protect Ian from his solitude. Ian is a lonely man, one of the loneliest I've met, because his situation forces him into a contemplative world to which he is unsuited.

Andy goes on every overseas trip with Ian, staying in one-night cheap hotels, rising early to drive his friend to his next destination. At first Andy was teased with being Ian's 'minder'. Then people realized that his role was far more important, far more significant than that humorous tag indicated. His job is to prevent Botham ever sinking into the defensive, lonely, depressed world inhabited by so many men too famous for their own good, too praised for their own sanity. Botham's faith in Withers is substantial and unshakable. And as Ian himself says, Andy would not betray him at any price: his loyalty is unquestionable.

His cricketing triumphs have brought Botham much wealth. He has a manager, an accountant, a gardener, a nanny, a companion, and a huge house. He drives a Jaguar, owns racehorses and gambles a lot. But what of the future? What happens next? In this final chapter Ian describes his vision of the future, and tries to explain his image. It is a sensitive subject.

Ian's Story

I will not be playing cricket in ten years' time. I won't be involved in the game at all. Some people cannot get away from it. Muhammad Ali made a fool of himself against Larry Holmes, hurting his reputation and his brain. His pride would not let him stop. It is easier if you are an actor, you can fit

140

snugly into older, more dignified roles. There is no such way out for someone involved in a physical thing like cricket. You can carry on, like Ray Illingworth or Bill Alley, until your pension is only fifteen years away, but you are bound to deteriorate. I've told myself not to allow this to happen. I want to leave head held high and to try other things while I'm still young. Peter May retired early, and so did Bob Willis. Once Bob felt he could not open the bowling for England he left the stage. I must do the same; once my powers begin to slip I must go. Maybe I'll try a season as a spinner or as a batsman, just for fun, but I won't hang around the edges of the game.

Already I am preparing for my retirement. I'm not a fellow to put my feet up, light a pipe, put on a pair of slippers and sit gazing at the fire. I'm not much use at home, sitting around. I want to fly aeroplanes, make films, reduce my golf handicap, breed horses and start a trout farm. Those are some of my ambitions, anyhow. Also I have an interest in a commercial radio station. There is such a lot to be done. It would be silly to ruin my reputation by hanging on like some old stager with nothing else to do. It suits some people – they love the game so much, they cannot imagine life without it. But I prefer to move – I don't want to get stuck in a rut, I don't want to spend the second half of my life reliving the first half. I don't want to end up telling people to bend their knees and to keep their elbows up. That is why the Tim Hudson episode began, I suppose. He seemed to offer new challenges, he was into bright clothes, rock music, films and the bright lights as well as cricket. He appeared to lead a really colourful way of life just at a time when I seemed to be surrounded by dull, dreary people worrying about how many pence they got per mile, that sort of stuff. Hudson was refreshing. Suddenly I saw an opportunity to combine my interests, to show people my full range.

Cricket has gone on as if people dance the tango when they go to discos. We will never attract the young that way. Most of our commentators are old-timers who continually refer to the past. You don't hear disc-jockeys on Radio One yammering on about the Syd Lawrence orchestra. Tim Hudson wanted to hear people say, when they saw me hit a six, 'Hey, did you see Bruce Springsteen behind that shot', not, 'Well he's slogged that one into the river'. There is a baseball commentator in America called Don Meredith, who used to play for the Dallas Cowboys. He dresses up in cowboy gear when he is on television and talks in terms of rock-and-roll. The others are intimidated by him, they daren't risk doing that. One of the problems with rock stars is that they get torn away from their roots. Blokes like Trevor Gard and Vic Marks, they're good friends of mine; I like playing with them, and I always will. Maybe we could travel around as a team playing games organized by aristocrats without losing our roots. Springsteen's done that; he has the same blokes around him as when he started, he still has the same mates and drinks in the same places. It is getting harder for him, especially as he plays huge stadiums now, not indoor venues. That is bound to distance him from his audience.

I like county cricket, though there is far too much of it. People who come to see Viv and I get short-changed sometimes because we are knackered before the game begins. I love the crowd, especially in Somerset where the support is terrific. Maybe some wealthy aristocrat can sponsor a team to travel around as W. G. Grace used to do, playing cricket privately and for money. One reason we have to play so much cricket in England is to deny us the time to organize private fixtures, I'm convinced of that. Instead of which the stars of the future will be driven away from the county game by so much being demanded of them for so little reward.

Athletics and tennis are already beyond the control of the authorities. Athletes like Coe and Ovett did not need to qualify for the British Olympic squad. They were put into an elite group, certain of selection irrespective of form. This was because the AAA cannot tell men like that what to do, where to run. There is too much at stake – and their careers are too short. In tennis the players stage a lot of exhibitions, travelling around the world playing in tournaments beyond the control of the international powers. McEnroe chooses to play in the US Open, and he chooses to play Wimbledon. He doesn't have to: his name, once it was made, could not be lost. His talent could have been squandered if he had played everywhere. Borg did that and realized it was killing his enthusiasm. He tried to reduce his tournaments but wasn't allowed to. He should have cut himself off from the authorities, like the professionals were cut off from the amateurs when it all started. Cricket's leading players are realizing the dangers of being burnt out, and of being exploited, and sooner or later they will organize themselves to stage matches besides those arranged by the ICC or whoever. I would lose a lot by leaving county cricket but, let's face it, I only play half the games as it is. The elite is nearly formed now, just as it is in Australia. Sheffield Shield and county cricket will soon be starved of stars, so that they will exist only as the sources from which the heroes emerge. It is bound to be so. International cricketers will lead a separate life from the treadmill of the county game. We'll have ten Tests against Australia, not five, and ten one-day games. Phil Edmonds says he'd like to play for England and Finchley. Pretty soon that is precisely what people will be doing.

I have been involved in advertizing for Shredded Wheat, Nike sports shoes, football boots, and Hamlet cigars. They portray me in a humorous way, and that's how I want to be presented – with a laugh, and with a message that says this fellow will do anything.

Often people are shocked when they meet me for the first time. They imagine I'm a madman who is likely to disappear for three days on a binge. I'm much sharper than they expect. I enjoy seeing the bewilderment on people's faces as they realize that this bloke isn't an idiot. It is good to be underestimated, so that you can rise up and amaze everyone, just as they are writing you off. To prove yourself once more is a challenge, especially as it leaves your critics with egg on their faces. Critical comments spur you on, give you extra motivation. Right, you say, I'll prove them wrong. When a game is dying and you get up each morning thinking what a damn nuisance it is that you've got to go to play cricket, you need these pinpricks to goad you on.

Sometimes I am asked why I shouldn't accept criticism if I'm playing badly, why I should expect to be immune. Well, to my mind it is a matter of faith. If you're in bad form for a while, people rush to condemn you. They fall over each other to do it. Their opinions change every day. They have no patience and no faith. Every bad patch is regarded as a sign that you are not trying, or that you are no good any more. But everyone has bad times and during these you cannot win. If you smile and go for your shots they say you don't care. If you put your head down and edge one to slip they say you'll have to go. Your critics forget their own bad times and the struggles they had.

As I said earlier, if you are written off it can fuel your determination. You go through a slump, and you can't help reading the papers. If you don't order them yourself someone will certainly send them along to you! These things light a fire inside you. When Ballesteros won the Open a couple of years ago I backed him. He'd had a terrible season and they said he had no chance. No one ever mentioned him as a threat. Men like that are at their most dangerous when they are down because they are brilliant and because they are fighters. Ballesteros played in a fury, and smashed the ball all over the place. He wins when he does that. When he tries to play safe, concentrating on hitting the fairway, then he's just the same as every other clockwork golfer. He is the sort of character I admire. John McEnroe too – he doesn't take any nonsense from anyone. He stands up for his rights, and expects the linesmen to be as good at their task as he is at tennis. He gets fed up with doddery old linesmen who are ruining his years of hard work by making mistakes. He's bad-tempered, of course, but that's a part of his talent, it is a part of his artistry. He gets frustrated when things go wrong; he is a touch player who is a genius when everything is working. Sportsmen, especially gifted ones, are not machines.

This is the sort of fellow I want to be in the public eye. I enjoy the 'mission impossible' side of things. I want to show the kids that they must give it a go, must never drop their heads. I love performing these great rescue acts, when suddenly everything is turned on its head. Maybe I go for those too often, but the kids watching must see a bold fellow who is not afraid, and perhaps some of them who are told to be careful, get their exams, improve their averages, take out a mortgage on a house, buy a nice little car and work in an office, will ignore the advice. Kids don't want to do all that but they are encouraged to do so by mediocre people in this dull world. Their spirit is taken out of them and they are filled with insecurity. If I'm any sort of hero, I want to be the type who tells them to ignore everyone and to go up a mountain, or down a river, or fight a war, or write a book, to do what ever they want to do and not to worry about things going wrong. If they copy me, and I hope some of them do, at least they will be neither timid nor tame.

This is where the headlines hurt. I'd like to be remembered as the fellow who never thought a cause was lost, as the fellow who did not run away from the toughest challenge. I don't want to be remembered as a bloke who had drugs in his house. Nor do I want to be remembered as the idiot who threw it all away. I've heard of cricketers, great players of their day, finding themselves in a gutter. This seems to have happened to West Indians and to Australians in particular.

I don't want to be a businessman because so many of those fellows in bowler hats and suits look terribly bored. I'd rather go around in my jeans and leather jacket and feel happy. I don't want to be an ant. On the other hand I have a wife and kids, and even though I don't really worry about tomorrow I will never let my family be destitute. Without being a squirrel, without refusing to do something because it costs too much, I have a certain amount set aside. You won't read about *this* former England cricketer being out on the streets with his wife and children, because he backed a few slow horses or thought red was bound to come up soon in the casino . . .

I enjoy the things cricket has brought me. Money isn't everything – I didn't join Packer and I didn't go to South Africa, despite massive offers. But wealth brings you a lot and I don't want to lose it. I realize this could happen, so I've learned to be a bit shrewd.

Cricket is a dangerous game and I don't blame those who do try to secure their futures. For most of them it is their only chance. It's easy for me to turn down an offer, or for you who has never received one, to tell everyone else they should! It isn't so easy for an ordinary cricketer. There was always a lot of hypocrisy around cricket and it hasn't vanished yet. A lot of pretty speeches were made about how terrible Packer was and yet these very critics were often the ones who were not looking after their players. Many cricketers don't have jobs during the winter, most have little in prospect after they are sacked or retire. Those who grumbled about Packer had created the circumstances in which he emerged, because they had failed in their responsibilities to their players. Packer made cricketers feel wanted, and he paid them their dues, something which the cricket boards had failed to do. A cricketer doesn't expect sympathy, he doesn't think of himself as an old farm-hand who has to be kept on even when he's broken down. He realizes that his value to his club is in the runs he scores or the wickets he takes but he'd like to feel that his employers take some interest in him. As it was, they paid him as little as possible and washed their hands of him when he left. The Packer rebellion was a good thing because it woke the authorities up, showed them that cricketers are not merely statistics, they are men with families, wives and all the rest of it.

On top of this, the cricketers, certainly the best ones, realized they did have some strength, and now they cannot be so easily intimidated. Cricketers don't walk about touching their forelocks or quaking with fear every time a committee man walks by or every time someone mentions the contracts meeting. In Somerset's team last summer we had three men from Oxford or Cambridge, one due to go there in September and a youngster who might be there in a year or two. Besides these we had a couple of others who could have gone to university, plus the captain of the West Indies, a former captain of England, and Joel Garner, who isn't exactly a fellow you can ignore. All these are men of calibre and not men who could easily be frightened. These are the people who should run the game.

Cricket has brought me everything I ever wanted. I suppose it happened too quickly in a way. I went from being a promising fellow to England's great hope in a single blink. Sometimes I am presented as England's only hope and people expect a great deal every time I play. During the last ten years, in which I've played almost without stopping, there have been times when I've played badly. Maybe it is not healthy to be in the spotlight all the time, maybe it breeds a certain arrogance beyond what a man needs if he is to succeed. If everyone is studying your every move, even when you go shopping, you are bound to conclude that you must be a hell of a fellow. Even if you weren't vain at the start, after ten years under the microscope you begin to suspect that there must be something interesting about you. Being a star is like living in a greenhouse. My home is not a castle you see – I cannot live like a W. G. Grace, or a Denis Compton – my home is a greenhouse.

It has been worth it, though: my only regret is that I spend so little time with my kids. I'm not finished yet. I want Somerset to win the championship and I want to be free to hit the ball. I never want to be inhibited, I never want to stop doing things. Neither in life nor in cricket do I ever want to half-hit shots.

CHAPTER THIRTEEN

New Horizons

A month after the publication of the hardback edition of this book, Somerset announced its decision to release Joel Garner and Vivian Richards from their contracts. At once, the book was examined for evidence predicting such a divide. In fact, work began on *It Sort of Clicks* in September 1984, at the end of Botham's first year as captain of Somerset. Because the book was about Botham's early career and the changes in his life, the dramatic events at Somerset (not anticipated when the words were written), did not much affect the content. Nevertheless, those were passionate times and the publication of this paperback edition gives me the opportunity to describe Botham's departure from Somerset and the other extraordinary changes in his life that took place in 1986. By chance the months from April 1986 to February 1987 were as vital to his career as any previous period. Around the time *It Sort of Clicks* was published in Australia, Botham left Somerset, his county for thirteen years, and signed for Worcestershire.

To understand properly how the Somerset affair began to build towards its ugly, fraught climax it would be necessary to trace the history of the club at least since 1 April 1974, the day Richards, Botham, Marks and Roebuck signed on. In *The Airman and the Carpenter* Ludovic Kennedy observes that cases cannot be understood without reference to the lives of the characters in the years before forces brought them together in mortal dispute. In his study of the kidnapping and murder of the Lindbergh baby and the subsequent, wrongful execution of Richard Hauptmann for the offence, Mr Kennedy traced the lives of the German illegal immigrant and the heroic pilot, set them against their times and showed how the conviction of Hauptmann had come about. To Kennedy the trial was simply the climax of a long historical process.

And so it is at Somerset. The decision and the meeting were not the beginning and the end of the matter, they were both a part of the final chapter. One day, maybe, a history will be written tracing the life of Viv Richards, from humble and proud origins on the backwater island of Antigua, of Botham as he rose from wild youth in Yeovil to greatness as a cricketer, and of the other characters in this history. It is not possible, here, to be so wide-ranging, nor to investigate those years, to see the forces of antagonism as they move, scarcely realising it, into conflict. This is not the place to study the decline of Somerset from the peaks of 1979 and 1981 through the first signs of trouble in 1982 when the poison began to creep into the body of the club, and onto the sad fall.

Instead, this last, extra chapter will describe Botham's season at Somerset in 1986, his part in the battle, his efforts in Australia, his choice of Worcestershire as his county for the second part of his career, and his decision not to tour with England next winter and to play, instead, for Queensland.

Ian's position at Somerset in 1986 was awkward. He'd expected to survive as captain notwithstanding the club's poor position in 1985 because he could see no other candidate ready to replace him. He regarded Vic Marks, who'd done well as his vice-captain in extremely difficult circumstances, as the only challenger, and he considered Vic to be too affable to be appointed as captain (I didn't agree, and had argued that he should be made captain in 1984). To his surprise he had been relieved of the captaincy and had been replaced by myself. We'd had an odd relationship over the years, a mixture of quiet affection, sympathy, occasional periods of true friendliness and chillier months in which, though still aware of the other qualities, faults appeared in vivid detail.

To add to Ian's woes, two of his chums, Richard Ollis and (to a lesser degree) Nigel Popplewell, had left the club. Reporting at Taunton for the first game, Botham found a collection of youngsters he scarcely recognised, of signings he'd never met to add to the few remaining old hands, some of them members of the inner circle with which this insecure man with a yearning to be wanted surrounds himself. He had only two or three bosom pals left, a worrying development for a man who fears isolation.

It will not benefit to record every little dispute during the season, for there are plenty of little disputes in any season, and to concentrate upon them is to distort the picture. Till the final break-up, Ian and I enjoyed a curious relationship in which we'd laugh in private and yet fight about the cricket. We were dedicated, I suppose, to different gods. I expected Somerset to play constructive, tight cricket, whereas Ian's entire career had been founded upon the untamed expression of flair. He wanted to charge the enemy (that is, on those occasions when he saw fit to join battle), whereas I wanted to develop strategies. Ian, used to being captain at Somerset, used to plotting his own course with England, may have surveyed my demands with a caustic eye. I, perhaps, felt he might have fitted in more readily to the collective approach.

However, these are minor matters. For the most part Botham and I got on well, and there was no question of Somerset rejecting Botham. In fact, the idea of tying him to a two-year contract before the overseas question was settled was contemplated, and then thrown out, as too disreputable a tactic. He was Somerset bred, if not born, and he was also a formidable, match-winning cricketer. His departure was not a part of the plan, though his intentions could not be allowed to affect the decision, which stood or fell on its merits. There never was any devious plan to nail Botham.

Such arguments as we had during the season were mere skirmishes, and no heed was paid to them. Far more typical was the efforts made by several people to protect Ian when he got into trouble. He had not been dismissed as captain when pleading guilty to possessing cannabis one winter and on several other occasions he had been stoutly defended. Soon another opportunity arose for those close to Ian to help him or to hurt him. As ever they fought by his side; if they'd wanted to lose him they'd never have done so.

It is not appropriate to define the matter that arose early in May 1986 to imperil Ian's career. Nothing could be worse than to put here something which was not, finally, carried in any newspaper. Suffice it to say that for a few days it appeared likely that further revelations about Ian's private affairs were to be published. For two or three days these latest allegations hung over Somerset cricket like the sword of Damocles. In the end the newspaper withdrew its story and Ian's friends could breathe a sigh of relief, happy that he would not be obliged to sue again to save his career. Botham has travelled near to the edges on several occasions but has probably never come so close to a fall before – a fall that, considering his character taken as a whole, he ill-deserved.

Ian's private life has never interested me in the slightest. He does, at least, bring life to a sometimes drizzly country. He is entitled to resent the way in which his life is so thoroughly investigated, though he is at least in part to blame for leading his life in so public a way. Sadly in this puritanical age the nocturnal antics of public figures are considered fair game. People can no longer work with whom they choose nor sup what they choose.

Unfortunately, the story which so nearly ruined everything was not the last of the season. On 18 May Ian announced, out of the blue, or so it appeared, in the *Mail on Sunday*, that he had, in his youth, smoked marijuana, or 'pot' as it was more melodramatically called in the headlines.

No-one at Somerset had any warning of this story, not so much through any rudeness on Botham's part as because the *Mail* could not keep its hot, exclusive tag and yet allow Botham to fulfill his obligation to inform the club of anything to be published under his name (players are contractually bound to submit their pieces to the censor at Lords – or to its representatives in the counties – to check that nothing is printed that is deemed to be damaging to the reputation of the game). Our game with Sussex being delayed till the Monday, Botham had mysteriously taken off to London. Later we realised that his purpose was to be photographed with Kathy, the happy couple sticking together in the hard times. The first I heard about Botham's sudden confession was on Saturday night when someone from the club, who'd been contacted by the paper, rang to recommend that I change my newspaper order for the following day.

According to the article, nominally written by Ian but really concocted with the help of solicitors and editors, Ian had misbehaved in a variety of ways in his youth. He vehemently denied any more recent involvement with drugs and spoke of his loathing for them. At once it was obvious that this article was not all it appeared to be. Why on earth would Ian make any such confession? Why would he change his tune so dramatically? For years he'd contemptuously and angrily denied any involvement in drugs at any time in his life, yet here he was apparently loading the guns of his enemies. Evidently he had not done this simply for the money.

In fact, Ian had pinned himself into a corner. The *Mail on Sunday* had published a series of allegations about Botham's conduct in New Zealand on the 1983–4 tour, and Botham had immediately sued for libel, a move which had the effect of squashing the stories by making them *sub judice* and yet opened up Ian's life to the scrutiny of investigative reporters. The *Mail* had scoured Botham's life, spending tens of thousands of pounds collecting evidence against him. Botham had taken on a giant, and he did not have the resources for the fight. The *Mail* was confident of winning the case and, perhaps reluctantly, of hurting Botham's standing once and for all. Few men's lives can bear so unsympathetic an examination. Few do not have something to hide, some vulnerability better hidden from the world. Botham, presumably, had rather more skeletons in his cupboard than most.

He'd been forced to find a way out of a case that was draining his funds and threatening to finish his career. The price exacted was heavy. Botham had to pay the costs of both sides – itself an awesome task –, had to drop his libel suits and had to write an exclusive article admitting that he'd smoked pot in his younger days. The *Mail on Sunday*, in its turn, shredded its files. It, too, had little appetite for the business. Botham had begun the action in haste, striking out to defend himself, and he'd paid for this gut reaction, paid for this panic as he saw his reputation being dragged down.

Ian's article did not at first strike people at Somerset as particularly objectionable. He had, in fact, conceded little ground. If every cricketer who had, at one time or another, tried marijuana in his youth were to be scratched from the game, counties might be hard pressed to raise satisfactory teams. Youthful indiscretions are not unique to Mr Botham. On the other hand, in the light of his repeated denials of any involvement he had, at least, shown an incomplete respect for the truth. Also he had failed to show the article to the proper authorities to be approved.

At once, reporters and television crews descended upon Somerset's hotel in Brighton. It began to seem as if Ian would forever be dogged by scandal. Certainly his last three years had been ridden with them. Apart from his dreadful troubles in the West Indies only a couple of months earlier, this was the second major Botham story of the season, and it was only the middle of May. These journalists were well versed in the routine of Botham stories. Failing to locate the principal actor they hung around the hotel, speaking to anyone remotely connected with the club, waiting for something to happen. I defended him largely on the grounds that he hadn't actually said anything and could not be convicted merely on the supposition that if he was guilty of this he was probably guilty of everything else.

This defence of Botham was sincere because in this instance he did appear more sinned against than sinning. He had taken on Fleet Street and in doing so he had got quite out of his depth. He did not have hundreds of thousands of pounds to spend. Moreover, as the song says, to live outside the law you must be honest. Do not fight the Street of Shame unless your conscience is as clear as spa water.

Botham returned to Brighton that night and we had a chat in the bar. I predicted he'd be punished, he believed he'd said nothing and would get off scot free. He thought he'd disentangled himself rather skillfully, though he was scarcely prepared to acknowledge any difficulty. It has to be said he is a man with an astonishing ability to rewrite the truth, not merely for public consumption, but for the satisfaction of his own memory. A table is not there because he can kick it; it is there if he says it is there. This is one of the characteristics that helped him rise in the game. He is not merely a cartoon character, he is the author of the cartoon.

Besides saying he'd done nothing wrong, Botham disappointed me by adding that if he was punished it was something he could exploit. Even this, it appeared, could be turned into an opportunity to be heroic. At this point I left him to it. Next day he was surrounded by photographers, cheered by the crowd, even though we lost the game.

Ian was suspended from first class cricket for two months, in part to encourage the others. Some people had wanted to ban him for life. One or two highly respected writers argued that he should never play Test cricket again. This was, I suppose, an older generation over-reacting. Botham had, still, only admitted smoking 'grass' in his youth. He could be punished for nothing else. Perhaps some people put marijuana in the dreaded company of heroin, LSD and cocaine, imbuing it with imaginary evils. Possession of it being illegal, Botham's conduct could not be condoned, even if it was only in his callow youth, but this was a time when the quality of mercy was not strained. Of course the publication of the article itself was another matter. It did appear as if the criticism of Botham were for things he was supposed to have done rather than charges proven against him.

Botham, after a period of contemplation, appealed against a sentence which, in fact, disrupted Somerset cricket as much as his life (the punishment evoked waves of sympathy). Somerset had been riding high in the championship and in the John Player League, but this excellent beginning could not be sustained after the Bath Festival in mid-June. The falling away, caused in part by Botham's absence, led to a decline in morale, nearly down to the levels of the previous four years. His appeal failed, Somerset lodged an appeal too and that also failed.

Nor was Ian's eight-week break without incident. He interrupted his fishing and flying to make an after-dinner speech in which he referred to the selectors as 'gin-soaked old dodderers'. This somewhat indiscreet description was recorded by an opportunist at the dinner and sent to a national paper, which gleefully printed the story. This was a sorry matter because Botham had been in humorous vein and because he had been carefully protected by several men on the selection panel, who were entitled to regard these remarks as a poor return.

The idea that Ian is picked upon by people in power is inaccurate. Ian is paid a large sum of money by one paper as a consequence of which the others chase him. It is a competition he entered freely and with his eyes open. Occasionally stories are thrust upon the authorities by investigative journalists writing for these rivals, and these stories are duly investigated. For the most part, though, those in charge of Ian would far rather not know what he or any other player gets up to in his spare time. Ian has been protected by his own. He is not an enemy to authority, but one of its most cherished sons, which is itself a tribute to the feelings of warmth which most colleagues have towards this man.

Ian's absence ended with a dramatic hundred at Weston-super-Mare, an innings which began his campaign to get back into the Test team and to secure his place for the Ashes tour to Australia. Gatting, determined to treat Botham as a cricketer rather than as a saviour, said that the all-rounder's selection was not certain. In fact, England had played mundane cricket all summer and Botham could not be ignored for the final Test against New Zealand.

Naturally he took a wicket with his first ball, an ordinary delivery outside the off-stump which the usually durable Edgar managed to edge to slip. Botham thumped the air as if to show the Doubting Thomases (he is often the man who sows those seeds of doubt). With the bat he scattered the fieldsmen, even those of Hadlee who had ruled the roost in England and in Australia since September. Botham was back, and once again writing his own headlines. He believes that, with these magnificent deeds, he can scatter all those unpleasant stories to the winds. As with his great walk, he is confident that one extraordinary feat will make up for lots of little misdemeanours.

Sadly, Ian will not remember this Test match for his return. On the third morning, a Saturday, Somerset announced that it had decided to release Joel Garner and Viv Richards and to offer Martin Crowe a contract. In the England dressing room Botham was shocked and at once began to ring friends in Somerset. From the start he plunged into the thick of the action just as he did on the field, rushing courageously as if into a scrum, fighting with every available weapon. At once he announced that he'd leave Somerset if this decision was not overturned and at once he began a vigorous campaign to gather the players and the public around him in order to defeat the club. He called the decision arrogant and ungrateful, regarded it as appalling and despicable. He announced his belief that blood was thicker than water and his wrath was evident. At home his friends were no less furious, a fury rising at times to venom. He opined that Somerset would be a laughing stock, and that it was doomed to sink to the depths. I argued that we were already there.

Ian returned to Taunton after the Test match to begin his campaign and to play in the county game against Essex, the championship leaders. From this point the cricket took a secondary place in the minds of the protagonists in the dispute at Somerset.

On the first night of the Essex game Ian called a meeting of all the professional players to which I was not invited. Throughout the meeting he referred to me as 'Judas', and later he hung a placard with this word upon it above my place in the changing room. He wanted to hold a vote of no-confidence in me but was dissuaded from doing so by other senior players, who urged him to keep out of the fracas as his threats would be resented by many people who remembered how much the club had stood by him. Curiously, Ian, a man immensely popular in England, was more remote from the Somerset people than Viv and Joel.

But Ian had the scent of battle and would not, could not, stop. His involvement changed the issue from whether or not the decision itself was correct to what sort of club the members wanted, irrespective of the merits of this particular decision. At first the case had been about the release of two distinguished and long-serving cricketers; now it was about tails wagging dogs.

Moreover, Ian's vitriolic attack upon myself forced me to join in the struggle and to articulate the club's case. Perhaps optimistically, I had intended to leave for Australia at the end of the season and let the indignant armies fight it out. I did not consider myself to be a central figure; however, I was not prepared to sit by in the face of bitter public attacks (of private assaults there had already been plenty).

For the next few weeks Ian pursued his course, urging on the players and spreading unpleasant rumours (of all people, he should have avoided this). Perhaps he damaged the dissenters' case by launching his crusade and by beginning this personal attack upon myself. At times I felt like a man who, with a six-shooter in his belt, is accosted by a gentleman with one bullet in his gun, and that a dud.

Yet, despite the methods used, Ian's stance was honourable in its way. He believed he was sticking by his mates who, he believed, had been poorly treated. He does not play his cricket according to the coaching manual and could not be expected to conduct this war of words as if he were in a polite debating house. He is such a mixture of good and bad and the two months at the end of an extraordinary incident-packed year showed him at his worst and his best.

Botham was in Australia at the time of the meeting and, though rumours indicated otherwise, he did not send any final message to the members. In fact, his name was scarcely mentioned at the meeting, a remarkable situation for a great cricketer who'd entered the fray with such force.

He heard the result over the phone and was devastated. In his press conference next day, he said he was sorry for Somerset, confirmed his determination to leave and announced, in an offhand way, that I'd be advised to stay in England rather than flying to Australia to see him. Actually, I was going to Australia to work for *The Sunday Times* and for the *Sydney Morning Herald*.

The conflict soon died during the tour. At first he thought some terrible disaster had befallen him. Gradually, he realised that he'd be happier at another county and that he had not really enjoyed himself at Somerset for several years. He'd lost contact with the grass roots at the club and did not really feel a part of things. Perhaps he understood, too, that his boredom with county cricket and his battles with authorities could have a detrimental effect upon others. A fresh start might do him good.

We met two or three times during the tour. The press stayed in the same hotels, flew on the same aeroplanes and inevitably our paths crossed from time to time, though with Ian staying in his hotel room and me leading an independent life we did not often bump into each other. When we did relations were cordial. We did not talk about the Somerset business because there really wasn't much point. His mind was made up.

His choice of Worcestershire as his next county was no surprise. He has so many friends there – committeeman Mick Jones and pace bowler Paul Pridgeon. He asked after the fishing (Botham has a genius for public relations which, with his courage and his fear of loneliness, is his most striking characteristic) and observed that Worcester was only 100 miles up the M5 so Somerset supporters could pile into coaches to go to watch him. On the day of his signing he told Derek Taylor, Brian Rose and Nick Pringle (Past, Present and Future), who happened to be in Sydney, that he'd already pencilled in the Somerset v Worcestershire game as a day of reckoning.

At once, Botham set about creating a set of friends at Worcestershire. In Australia his biggest chums were Graham Dilley and Phillip deFreitas. By the end of the tour Dilley had been persuaded to join him in Worcester. This was the old fear at work. If one set of friends had rejected him, why he'd simply create another. Ian wants not to be judged but to be loved, as a child can be in a family.

It was strange, though, that Worcestershire was the only county to offer Botham terms. Here was the greatest entertainer of the age, one of the greatest match-winners in the game and yet only one of fifteen counties dared to offer him terms. Maybe the others recognised that they really didn't have a chance. Botham's future was already a foregone con-

clusion. He had not the slightest intention of going to Derby-
shire or to Gloucestershire. At Worcestershire he was joining
some bosom pals, was keeping within striking distance of
Taunton and was playing in a strong team. It was, in every
respect, a fortuitous move.

Given fresh purpose by these battles, determined to win back
his public, rejected for only the third time in his career (he'd
been sacked as captain by England and by Somerset), Botham
steeled himself to succeed in Australia. Stung by the scandals,
he paid for large suites in every hotel on tour and secluded
himself in them; these rooms became a gentleman's club
through which his closest friends passed (including Mr Elton
John, who followed the England tour for much of its course,
strengthening his close friendship with Botham).

He wanted to win the Ashes tour, not least because this was
to be the last tour for at least three years. For several years he'd
planned to withdraw from the cycle of a summer's cricket in
England followed by a winter's tour. He'd enjoyed his break in
1984–5 and he yearned for a life as far as possible away from
the hotel-foyer existence of a touring cricketer. He'd had
enough of all that. This tour of Australia was to be his last tour
till the next trip downunder. He'd no longer be at the beck and
call of the selectors. This had been his plan for some time.
Botham plans his career far more carefully than he cares to
pretend.

During the winter, and to no-one's surprise, Botham
announced that he intended to spend the next three seasons
playing state cricket for Queensland. His choice of state pro-
vides another clue to the character of this cricketer. Botham is
close friends with Allan Border (one of those who visited Ian in
his hotel kingdom). These two men are essentially unpretentious, pragmatic and earthy. They are both weary with formal-
ity and with committee rule. Border is a simple man and a
gritty cricketer who takes pride in playing for Australia. He
may be disconcerted by Botham's more idiosyncratic deeds but

he warms to him. Significantly it is Botham who has gone towards Border, searching for a home in his neighbourhood, as a cold man searches for a log fire.

Jeff Thomson is a mate too, another chum to lure Botham towards the vast, hot and empty state north of New South Wales. Thomson is a larrikin and a raconteur, a man who is game for a laugh, a man who has never taken the game or its authorities too seriously. To Botham's amusement, Thomson is currently doing well as a landscape gardener (though it is not clear if he has yet landscaped gardens other than those of Allan Border, Greg Ritchie and, I daresay, Greg Chappell). 'Thommo' has all the qualifications to be a soul partner for Ian Botham.

Queensland has never won the Sheffield Shield, despite importing expensive cricketers like Chappell, Border, Thomson and Botham. This failure is partly caused by the tropical weather which can ruin games in Brisbane after the turn of the year. Presumably even Ian will be unable to stop the thunderstorms. Despite this problem, Queensland reached the Shield finals in 1985 and 1986, only to lose both, one in a breathtaking finish at the SCG against New South Wales. Botham may well succeed in rectifying this position and if he does so he will be lauded in this deeply conservative, rural state.

He may, perhaps, hope to avoid some of the bugbears of stardom by going to Queensland. Perhaps he hopes to collect his money, enjoy his life and be free from the caresses of *The Sun* and the stings of its rivals. If he entertains any such optimistic thoughts he is being naïve. Papers have their stringers in Brisbane, and Botham is too embedded in the editorial rooms to escape now. He's embraced stardom wholeheartedly and he is stuck with it. He will, though, have plenty of days off on which to pursue his enthusiasm for hunting and fishing and he will not, at least, be spending his time in an hotel room, however pleasant. It is something.

Ian did play well on the Ashes tour, and England did hold on to the little urn. England won two Test matches and in both games Botham performed well. In Brisbane he struck a considered and finally thunderous hundred which destroyed the cocky spirit with which the Australians had begun the game. Suddenly thrown onto the back foot by an England team written off by the critics, the Australians lost the game and gave England a lead that was never relinquished. Botham's hundred, psychologically vital, was a measured innings of the highest quality. He'd set himself to reach three figures and he did so. He is a man of immense will who rarely falls short of his goals.

In Melbourne, returning from an injury sustained during the second Test in Perth, Botham struck again. Bowling off a few paces and still handicapped, he took five wickets as Australia fell for a paltry score, to give England the game and the series. Botham had been in the centre of the two telling sessions in the series. In truth the Australians batted recklessly, swishing wildly in pursuit of Border's instruction to risk all in attack. Nevertheless, Botham, mixing up his little swingers with sharp changes of pace, was the bowler who undid them.

He did not contribute much in the other three games. Statistically he did not have a particularly good series, one big innings and one haul of five wickets. In fact he exerted a considerable influence over the games, catching well at slip and looming over proceedings as a volcano looms over a nearby village. He missed the game in Adelaide and at once Gatting and his team scurried onto the defensive, as if alarmed at the prospect of encountering a none too formidable Australian eleven without the help of the bulldog Botham.

Most significantly of all, Botham contributed throughout to the team effort. For years, certainly since those magical and delusory Tests in 1981, England had relied too much on Botham's flair. Here Gatting insisted that Botham work hard in the nets, field with the rest of the players before each day's cricket and bowl as instructed. Botham was treated not as a wayward genius but as a part of a team effort. This approach worked superbly, and far from pouting, Botham simply got on with his job. Gatting used Botham's talent wisely, and did not allow his forceful personality to dominate the party. He was straight and demanding, and from first to last he was in charge. It was an impressive performance made possible by the degree of friction between these two abrasive cricketers. Gatting proved to be a match for Ian, and he led the team very well. He was the best and least indulgent captain Ian has had, at least since 1981. Botham's qualities did not run beside those of the team, they were incorporated as part of the general strategy.

Playing thoroughly professional cricket, England won The Ashes, and a small tournament in Perth in which they beat the West Indies, Pakistan (twice) and Australia to boot. They won the World Series Cup too, beating the West Indies and Australia to complete a remarkable and unsuspected treble. Botham, whose record in one-day internationals is not impressive (batting average of 22 and no hundreds) and who did not play well in the qualifying matches, lifted his game in the final with some vigorous hitting to give England a 2–0 victory and a few days on the beach before the long flight home. These final victories confirmed the authority of Peter Lush, Mickey Stewart and Mike Gatting, confirmed the ability of this England team and made everyone wonder what on earth has been going on in English cricket this last five years that England arrived in Australia as, perhaps, the worst Test team in the world. They left with respectable claims to be the best.

It was a satisfactory winter for the England team. It was a satisfactory winter for Botham too, particularly after the various misfortunes of the summer months. At the end of the tour he could look forward not to another season at his old club but to fresh challenges in Worcester and in Brisbane. After a wretched year his life had taken a turn and by January the bitterness and the tension had been left behind and replaced by a sense of wonder at what the future might bring. Consequently, we parted cordially too, the battles of the past not having entirely destroyed our relationship.

This is not the definitive book on Botham, was not meant to be. It began as a combined effort and ended, in this chapter, with the parties divided. One day someone will write a biography of Botham good enough to stand on the record as the mark of the man. This will not be done for five years, may not be done for ten years. At present we still need a little distance and a little time to assess the cricketer who is, and may continue to be for some time to come, difficult, outrageous and extraordinary.

Index